Liquid thinking
Damian Hughes

Introduction

Having read this book, I am flattered that I have been presented as a role model and am delighted to be asked by Damian to offer a foreword for 'Liquid Thinking'.

As someone that has achieved many of my own personal goals and experienced the satisfaction from doing so, I would recommend that you adopt the lessons and techniques, which are captured in this excellent book, to greatly assist you in achieving your own ambitions.

Go ahead. Take the plunge and become a fellow liquid thinker.

Sir Richard Branson

Foreword

Angelo Dundee is the best know of all boxing trainers. He is the most recognisable and famous. He trained over 15 world champions, including Muhammad Ali and Sugar Ray Leonard.

It gives me tremendous pleasure to be able to offer a contribution to this excellent book.

I have been involved with boxing for 57 years and have been fortunate enough to train and work closely with over 15 world champions, including some of the all-time greats like Muhammad Ali and Sugar Ray Leonard. It is for this reason that I feel able to comment upon what makes the difference between the ordinary and the great, where the thin dividing line between success and failure lies and what separates the true champions from the contenders.

It is not purely talent. I have seen hundred's of talented fighters who have never achieved everything that they should have done. It is not down to luck. Luck can only carry you so far. It is not about how privileged your background is or where you come from. It is about your attitude, the mental approach which you choose to adopt to chase your dreams. Damian has done a remarkable job in capturing, in this book, the tips and techniques which the great people, like Muhammad Ali, knew about and used to perfection to be able to conquer the world.

Your ambitions may be more moderate than that but it still shouldn't stop you using the same methods of the greats to help propel you towards your own goals. Combine these with the determination to work hard and dedicate your whole self towards achieving whatever it is you desire and you, too, can become your own version of a world champion.

Good luck.

Angelo Dundee

Contents

Why read this book?

I have written this book for a number of reasons. The main one being that I have always wanted to write one and I was determined to fulfil that particular ambition. The book which you now hold in your hands is the fulfilment of one of my goals and I hope that you will give it some attention.

The second reason is because I am a genuine believer that we are all capable of more than we give. I, therefore, wanted to write a book that was a celebration of those we work alongside every day, as well as famous and well known achievers; people that have given so much of themselves to achieve their own goals.

The final reason, is that I wanted to find out what these people have in common; what characteristics they share and what lessons and advice they could give that would allow others to learn from and go on to achieve their own special goals.

It is this reason that I wanted to write this foreword and I would offer two pieces of advice before you venture much further into this book.

1. Come along with an open mind. If I am right, think about what you have to gain. If you are determined to shoot down the lessons within the book and find fault, then I have no doubt that you will be successful. I also have no doubt that you will gain nothing from it. I'd advise you, therefore, to open your mind.

2. Have a pencil with you when you read. This book is yours, so feel free to sit with a pencil and annotate or highlight any passages which strike a chord with you. There are actions for you to take at the end of each chapter. Take time to work on each action. You may struggle with some of them at first. Don't worry, you can come back to it (skip to the chapter called 'Swim against the tide' if you really need some convincing!) but do take action to get the absolute most out of this opportunity.

The book is called 'Liquid Thinking'. Applying the lessons that can be learnt from 'Liquid Thinking' to your life, goals and ambitions will open up a world of opportunities. Go on, have a go. What have you got to lose?

I look forward to hearing about your successes in applying 'Liquid Thinking' and including them in the next volume.

Sink or swim

"No matter what your age, you are responsible for your own actions, irrespective of the actions or inactions of anybody else. If you are past the age of legal reason, you and only you are accountable for what you do or what you don't do".

Jerry Springer

Jerry Springer, eh? And you thought that this book would be containing quotes from loads of famous dead people? Well, in my view, his words are really relevant to this book and, most importantly, to you.

It is often said that there are three types of people in the world:
• those that make things happen;
• those that watch what happened;
• and those that say "what happened?"

In my job as an HR Manager, I am constantly amazed and fascinated by the amount of people who either consciously or unconsciously believe in fate. What do I mean by that? Try it yourself and listen to your colleagues and your mates talking and count how many "if only..."'s you hear in a day.

"If only the managers here knew how good I am...if only people would realise how talented I am...if only I had more money... if only I were a bit younger...if only I were older...if only I was in charge around here... if only people would listen to me... I'd be more successful".

Count how many times you hear yourself saying it (or words to that effect) and think instead about how much energy you are using to moan and what you could be using it for instead.

Woody Allen said that the world is run by people who turn up and when you talk to any successful person, they all say that, in life, there are either results or excuses.

The writer, George Bernard Shaw says:

"People are always blaming circumstances for what they are. I don't believe in circumstances. The people who get on in this world are the people who get up and look for the circumstances that they want...and if they can't find them, they make them."

Take, for example, Richard Branson, who found the right circumstances to build a business. He decided to set up his Virgin Atlantic airline after he had tried to book a flight to New York and had spent a morning hitting a redial button on the phone, as the only current company doing flights to America was constantly engaged. How many of us would find ourselves cursing and getting frustrated? Instead, he saw only an opportunity. He reasoned that the company was either very poorly managed, in which case it would be an easy target for new competition or that it was so much in demand, there was room for new competition. He saw a result not an excuse to give up trying.

Literally everything you do and everything you are - from how much money you earn, where you work, how successful you are as a parent, a friend, a workmate, where you live – is a direct result of decisions which you have made. Picking up this book and reading up to this word, is a decision made by you. I would, therefore, encourage you to make the decision to read further, where I have written about lessons which can be learned from meeting and reading about successful people, including our own North West Liquids employees, and put it into a structure that will make you think and will help you achieve what you really want.

Viktor Frankl was a Jewish prisoner who survived the Nazi's concentration camps but saw his wife and children killed in the camps. He has written a book about his experiences and talks about how he was forced to face the worst possible circumstances which you could imagine but he still believed that he had a choice. The only thing which the Nazi's could not take from him was his own attitude. It was a deliberate decision of his that they would not dictate how he felt. He could choose that. He says:

"We who lived in concentration camps can remember the men who walked through the huts comforting others, giving away their last piece of bread. They may have been few in number, but they offer sufficient proof that everything can be taken from a man but one thing: the last of the human freedoms - to choose one's attitude in any given set of circumstances, to choose one's own way."

If that powerful message isn't enough to persuade you to choose your attitude, there is another good reason. You will get to live longer. Now you may respond to this by arguing that there is no way that taking responsibility for yourself and your circumstances can influence this, that there are lots of variables that come into play: diet, work pressures, diseases and so on. So where could you do a study where everyone was submitted to the same environment? How about a convent?

A group of psychologists analysed the attitude of nuns before they entered a convent. They discovered that 90% of the nuns who took personal responsibility for themselves and their lives were still alive at 84. In contrast, only 34% of those who didn't accept full accountability were alive.

Finally, if Jerry Springer is a little too low-brow for you, I will finish off this chapter by quoting from another notable philosopher, Oprah Winfrey:

"My philosophy is that not only are you responsible for your life, but you are responsible for doing your very best at it at this very moment, which will put you in the best place for the next moment".

Do you choose to sink or swim?

Action:

Start to accept that you are 100% accountable and responsible for you and your life, your feelings and for every result which you get.

Stop making excuses and start to believe that you are the cause rather than the effect.

In 1964, when the Russian leader Nikita Khrushchev was removed from power, he sat and wrote two letters, which he handed to his successor, Brezhnev. He told him, when you get yourself into a situation which you are struggling to get out of, open the first letter. If it happens again, open the second one. Sure enough, trouble soon started to brew and eventually the new leader, Brezhnev, remembered the advice and sat and opened up the first letter. In it, it read 'blame everything on me.' And so, he told everyone that it was the fault of the old guy, Khrushchev and the crisis died down and soon passed. Shortly afterwards, when another row threatened and trouble flared up again, he remembered how effective the advice had been and so sat and opened the second letter. This one said 'start writing two letters.'

Don't blame others.

Accept personal responsibility.

Are you a drifter?

"We are each gifted in a unique and important way. It is our privilege and adventure to discover our own special light".

Mary Dunbar

When you go to a funeral, do you ever find yourself thinking about your own funeral and about how many people would come and who would be there? If you don't end up dismissing these thoughts from your head as morbid or depressing, do you ever think about the funeral in a bit more detail and imagine what people would be saying about you? What do you think your family, your mates and your work colleagues would say about you? Stop for a second and think about it.

Beyond the usual comments about being great fun, always standing your round and being a good husband/wife/dad, etc. do you think that anyone would be able to say what your purpose was? Why you were put here on the earth.

Wayne Bennett, a legendary Australian rugby league coach, summed it up well when, before a State of Origin match, which is the sporting series of Australia, he would challenge his players to train and play as well as they possibly could, in order to fulfil the purpose which they had been assigned and which they were born to meet, with the words:

"Don't die with the music in you!"

What a brilliant phrase that is. What do you think is the 'music' in you?

The psychologist, Sigmund Freud called our purpose, 'the golden seed'. Most successful people remember, at some stage in their formative years someone, somewhere telling them that they had a special talent. It can be a teacher, sometimes a first boss, a priest, occasionally a relative, sometimes a mother or father. They tucked this private nugget away in their heart but, in times of doubt or uncertainty, they pulled it out to reassure themselves that they were, indeed, pursuing their purpose.

Lance Armstrong, fell in love with cycling at the age of fifteen, influenced by his mother, who wanted him to keep fit and active. Richard Branson, one of Britain's most successful entrepreneurs, discovered his talent when he started a school magazine with some mates. For Muhammad Ali, it was his anger at feeling powerless to stop his bike being stolen by bigger, stronger kids which led him to a boxing ring where he was encouraged by his local police officer. For Tim Waterstone, the founder of the famous book stores, it was a fascination for marketing along with his interest in books which fired his passion for bookselling. Thomas Edison, the inventor of the lightbulb, was called "a stupid, muddle-headed blockhead" by a teacher at school. It was his mother who recognised his 'golden seed' and she went to the school and told the teachers that her son possessed real intelligence.

He said:

"she cast over me an influence which has lasted all my life. The good effects of her early teachings and belief I can never lose. My mother never misunderstood or misjudged me."

We all have a purpose which is unique to us alone. So how do you discover your purpose?

Here are a few suggestions for you to think about:

Don't mistake your job and your purpose as being the same thing.

Your job shouldn't define you. It should only support and link in with your purpose but should not be it. After all, what would you do if your job suddenly changed or disappeared? Think about how many people you know who have used the motivator of redundancy or retirement as a catalyst to go and do what they have always wanted. Your job should support what you have always wanted to do.

Richard Branson believes that "If you are working for what really matters – your purpose - you will give it all you've got".

Don't mistake your relationships as your purpose.

Don't get me wrong. This is not advocating that you leave your partner but think of the film 'Shirley Valentine'. She knew that her marriage did not fit with her purpose in life and so she fled to Greece to try and find it. Your relationship should be consistent with your destiny but should not be it. After all, a shared purpose is going to be even more powerful.

Do your goals fit with your purpose?

I will write about goals in a later chapter but what you do on a day-to-day basis should fit with your purpose. Do you find that you get easily caught up tackling problems for others rather than being able to devote time to yourself and your purpose? Success is not the result of luck or spontaneous combustion. You must first set yourself on fire. Instead, are you too busy putting out fires to be able to start any of your own?

It doesn't have to be an overtly impressive purpose.

Your purpose doesn't have to be all about resolving world peace or about curing cancer (you are not a Miss World contestant) so don't feel a need to invent something that is. It only has to impress you alone.

Your purpose doesn't have to make you a martyr.

A similar point to the last one. Your purpose should fit you like a glove and should not be governed by what others think of it. You are going to be the person living it and so if it excites you, that is all that counts.

Don't make your purpose complex.

Keep it simple and let it say something that stirs your soul and helps you to realise what it is you are here to achieve.

Jack Welsh, the former head of General Electric, who retired in 2001 after turning it into the world's most valuable company, said:

"Good business leaders also create a purpose, articulate this purpose, passionately own it and relentlessly drive it to completion".

You, too, should aim to stop drifting and have a clear purpose about what your life means and be able to explain what you are here to achieve.

A great example of someone who discovered what their purpose is, is the 7-times Tour de France winner, Lance Armstrong. At the age of 24, he was diagnosed with testicular cancer and doctors gave him only a 40% chance of survival. He said:

"If children have the ability to ignore all odds and percentages, then maybe I – we all – can learn from them. When you think about it, what other choice is there than hope. In that situation, we all have two options, medically and emotionally: give up or fight like hell."

The evening before he was due to have brain surgery, Armstrong was forced to think about his own death, which was frighteningly real. He says that it was on this evening, when he recognised his own purpose in life.

"I believed in belief, for its own shining sake. We are so much stronger than we imagine and belief is one of the most valiant and long-lived human characteristics. To believe..., that is a form of bravery. Without it, we would be left with nothing but an overwhelming doom, which will beat you."

His purpose wasn't to win cycling races – they were his goals - but, by winning them, he proved that the power of belief can overcome the most difficult circumstances.

After he had learned to recognise this he went on to win the gruelling Tour de France on a record seven consecutive occasions. When he first won it in 1999, he told the world media:

"When you get a second chance in life for something, believe in it and you will go all the way. I am proof of that".

What is your purpose?

Action:

"Here is Edward Bear coming downstairs now, bump, bump, bump on the back of his head, behind Christopher Robin. It is, as far as he knows, the only way of coming downstairs, but sometimes he feels that there really is another way, if only he could stop bumping for a moment and think of it".
Winnie the Pooh.

This quote is a great example of our everyday lives. We are having to move so fast just to get by that we never get the chance to stop and think about what we do and why we do it. Please take the time to stop and answer these questions which will help you to identify what your purpose is:

What are the 7 things you love to do?

1.

2.

3.

4.

5.

6.

7.

What are the 7 things that you are really good at?

1.

2.

3.

4.

5.

6.

7.

What do you consider is essential for you to do in life?

If you won the lottery, what are the 3 things that you would do?

1.

2.

3.

If you were writing your own obituary to be read out at your funeral, what would you want it to say?

Now write what your purpose is:

Liquid thinkers

Andy Hardcastle is an engineer in North West Liquids.

Imagine the scene. It's a crisp, cold winters' evening where you can see your breath forming in front of you in the clear, clean air as you sit at the wheel of your converted 1950 series 1 Land Rover in the middle of the beautiful Trentham countryside.

You flex your fingers around the steering to maintain the circulation and gently shake your head to ensure that the muscles in your neck and shoulders stay relaxed so that you can maintain your focus and concentration. It's been a long, drawn out day since you woke this morning and competed in the first race at 8.00am.

You clear your mind of tiredness and fix your full focus onto the section of the course which you are now required to tackle. You heard the muttered comments from the spectators about it being "impossible" and you make a deliberate effort to ignore them and block these negatives thoughts out of your mind and instead turn them into positives. It isn't impossible. It's tough, sure, but you are in the final of the British Land Rover Championship. You don't expect it to be easy.

This is the second head-to-head challenge that you have had to complete in the last few hours in order to be crowned as champion. The day had started out with 300 Land Rovers competing in the trial. The aim of the competition is to drive your vehicle over a difficult terrain, up steep hills, down fierce dips and through seemingly impossible angles as you weave through a course that is set up like a skiing slalom run. You lose points depending on how much contact you make with the wooden markers which mark the way. I had lost only 3 marks all day and now, after 12 sections and two individual duels, there was still no room to fit a cigarette paper between myself and Alex Skidmore.

The horn sounded to signal the start of my latest trial and although my neck, shoulders and body ached with the strain of pushing and pulling my 270 horse powered machine to its absolute maximum, my mind was fixed firmly on getting round with a perfect score. I manage it. I know I'm on fire and I know that I will not, I cannot, be beaten today.

When my rival again faces the same slalom and matches my achievements for the third time, I pulled up alongside him. We looked at each other and smiled. "Nothing's going to separate us today, is it?' I asked. "What do you think about us sharing this title?" He didn't say a word. Just extended his hand and we shook. At that moment, I became the joint 2004 British champion. My finest and greatest achievement.

Liquid thinkers

I've always been competitive in anything I do. I found the best outlet for my competitive nature at 16 when I started taking part in motorcycle trials. I progressed through the domestic ranks and eventually became regarded as a good club man at national level. I won a few 1st and 2nd class awards and even had a sponsor for a couple of seasons. I loved the challenge of pitching your skills and abilities up against another man and then seeing who could come out on top. I despair these days when I hear about schools trying to remove competition from the classroom and preaching to the kids that there is no winning or losing. That's life, isn't it? It's not about getting beat, it's all about what you take from a loss and learn from it.; what are the positives you can understand from it. During the years when I competed on the motorbikes,

this was my attitude and I loved the lessons it taught me in work and in life, in general.

As I got into my late 40's, I noticed that I was starting to get more injuries and that it was taking me longer and longer to recover from them, which included a total of 9 broken collarbones! I wanted to start looking at new horizons and new challenges. A mate of mine suggested that we went down to a local Land Rover club show in Wales for a laugh and when I watched it, I started to think that this would be a perfect sport which I would be able to do in my dotage. Plus, I've noticed that as men start to get older, they start to need bigger toys to play with. These huge beasts, which were being flung around the muddy, deeply rutted tracks with, what looked like reckless abandon, looked big enough for me!

I bought myself a 2nd hand Land Rover 1955 Series 1 to be able to start competing. I entered my first competition in Wales with a massive amount of enthusiasm. I couldn't wait to get started.

I came last, by quite some distance.

My attitude to this was helped by the lessons I'd learned during my earlier career on two wheels. Rather than get despondent and beat myself up about it, I asked plenty of other people for their help and advice and they were only too happy to help. They would suggest improvements which I could make to the car and slowly, I started to see my results improve.

A couple of years before I went on to win the British Championship, I achieved another personal ambition at Trentham Gardens in 2002. I'd always said that I wanted to go through a whole trial course without losing any marks. It's a tough challenge and I'd gone close a couple of times but I had noticed a pattern that after a lunch break, my concentration and focus dipped by 1-2% and this tended to be when silly mistakes cropped up and points were lost. On this day, I had a faultless morning and at lunchtime, I kept myself apart from everyone else and monitored the thoughts in my own head, ensuring that only positive messages, such as how well I was doing and how good a driver I was were in my mind. When I returned behind the wheel, I was feeling great and flew through the first section without any errors. I knew I could do it.

On the very last section, I was faced with a difficult uphill finish. I told myself that if I stuck to the same principles, I could do this. I measured the gaps and angles – using my Lever-issued tape measure! – and kept my Land Rover in a high gear with the clutch disengaged, my signature move. I flew up the hill and maintained my composure and concentration right to the very last second and landed right between the finishing canes.

The stewards seemed to take an age to determine whether I'd scored a flawless round but when they gave the signal to indicate that I had, I sounded my airhorn to signal my absolute joy. The other competitors heard this and understood. They joined in the chorus. At that minute, with the noise sounding like the Mersey on New Years' Eve, I thought back to my first race, when I trailed in last and remembered my positive attitude and the lessons I had learned.

I have had some tough times in competition. One year, I counted that I'd managed 18 complete revolutions as I turned the car over on numerous occasions. One time, after a particularly bad roll, I detached my retina and lost my sight for 3 days. That's why these days, I wear a helmet and have earned myself the nickname of 'Biggles'.

I'd encourage anyone reading this book to do your best in whatever you do and enjoy it. I've seen father's shouting at their kids during motorbike trials and it always strikes me that they are taking the fun out of the whole thing. You must enjoy what you do. That's the important thing.

Don't aim to be perfect. Why not aim instead to be excellent? There are some courses where I know that I'm not going to get a clean score. Instead, I aim for the next best option. If I aimed for perfection, I might as well never bother to start.

Finally, set your sights high. Don't just aim to be the best in your locality. Look for who is the best person you know and measure yourself against them. If you are going to compete, you may as well try to be the best you possibly can.

Thirst for success

"I dream, I test my dreams against my beliefs, I dare to take risks and I then execute my vision to make my dreams come true".

Walt Disney

Did you know that in 1928 when Walt Disney was only 26 years old, he was on the train from New York back to Kansas, when he drew a cartoon of a mouse on his sketchpad? Convinced that this drawing had the potential to be a success, he decided that he wanted to use it in a new form of film that had started to emerge called animation. In 1926, silent cartoons were still the only form of cartoon being produced but Walt had the dream that he wanted his mouse to feature in the first cartoon which featured sound. In order to achieve this, he needed to raise approximately $15,000 to make it. In today's money, this would be about $1 million.

Now put yourself in the shoes of a New York bank manager and imagine that you are sitting at your desk opposite a 26 year old lad who is asking you for a $1 million loan in order to make a new type of film, which doesn't even exist yet, but it involves a mouse. He has no real track record of success and has no savings of his own, which he can use to offset the risk. What would you say? Think about it.

Like you probably would, Walt's bank manager laughed him out of the bank.

Still, he didn't let this stop him and undeterred, Walt popped along to another bank to present his plan and request the money. He received a similar reaction to his first visit and so he popped to another, and another, and another, and... Are you starting to get the idea?

Stop again and now imagine yourself in the same situation as Walt Disney. How many banks do you think that you would have visited, receiving a mixture of negative, hostile and bemused reactions before you would have given up and thought of something better to do? One? Two? Ten? Twenty?

Walt Disney visited 305 banks before he found one which was prepared to take a gamble on him. He had a thirst for success and knew what he wanted to achieve and he was prepared to pursue it relentlessly, whatever the cost.

It has been proven, in numerous studies, that successful people have got a really clear and defined vision of what they want to do with their lives. They possess a crystal clear goal that lets them chase their passion rather than chase their pension. The fact is, though, how many of us have ever stopped the "bump, bump, bump" of life (which Winnie the Pooh spoke about in the last chapter) and given any thought about what we want out of life and what it is we need to achieve to be successful in fulfilling our purpose.

You have understood your purpose, now let us examine what it means to be successful. Winston Churchill thought that success was about being able to go from "one disaster to another without any loss of enthusiasm" until we achieve what we want (305 banks, remember!)

I suppose that success is different for all of us but there are some basic definitions by which we can identify what success is.

Success should be seen as a journey, not just a destination.

When Jack Dempsey retired as an undefeated world heavyweight champion, he was asked what it had felt like to achieve his ambition. Dempsey had grown up as a homeless kid and had become champion during the great Depression of the 1920's. He viewed his purpose as being someone who gave hope to others. He said:

"Becoming heavyweight champion of the world was the culmination of a dream but I loved the whole journey I made along the way".

It should be a pleasure to pursue your purpose not a chore or a task and it shouldn't be just about you getting to the point of success. The process of getting there should be enjoyed.

This reminds me of a great speech which Edward B Nervill, who was the vice president of General Motors, gave, just before he retired.

"Let us a recognise a basic truth. Success in life is not a destination. It is a journey. Fortunately, this means that no-one is obliged to work towards a single, distant goal and be judged successful only if he attains that one objective. As with a traveller, the end of the journey is usually beyond the range of vision but there is much of interest and beauty along the way to reward each day's steps. The happiest journey is not made with downcast eyes which see only tired, dusty feet. It is made with uplifted sight to appreciate its significance and to picture what may be beyond. The stars were made for those who look up and whose imagination knows no limits.

When I am feeling sorry for myself, I simply go for a walk and I keep on walking and walking, looking around me as I go – at the front doors that hide other people's fears and joys, at the marvels of nature, at the courage and invention behind every church and factory, at the sheer size and complexity of the small part of the world my legs can cover. And if that doesn't make my worries seem insignificant by comparison, I get rat-arsed!"

Success should be the realisation of your dream.

The more you focus and think about your purpose on the inside, the more it materialises on the outside. In other words, if it can exist in your head and heart, you should be able to hold it in your hands and know when you have attained it.

Imagine being Walt Disney on November 19th 1928 holding a copy of the New York Times which contains a review of Steamboat Willie, the first speaking cartoon, which premiered the previous evening and which described it as "ingenious and a good deal of fun". That idea had been in your head on the train journey when he had first drawn Mortimer Mouse (who later became Mickey) 2 years earlier and now it's success could be held in your hands. That is a realisation of a dream.

Success should be a worthy goal.

It should be a goal which you are in love with and enjoy chasing. Don't ask if you are capable or worthy of it but ask whether it is a goal which is worthy of you and your efforts.

When speaking about her work to set up a home to care for street children, Mother Theresa of Calcutta explained that "the success is in the loving, not in the result of loving".

A young Sven Goran Eriksson regularly visited England when he started coaching in Sweden and he studied the training methods of the leading coaches of the day and spent some time with Bob Paisley, the legendary Liverpool manager. He remembers vividly seeing Paisley dancing around on the touchline after a Liverpool goal:

"In that moment, I had a glimpse of what makes him tick. Here was a man so passionate and in love with the game and obsessed with winning".

Paisley himself agreed:

"I hear and read about what makes a successful manager but it is the same for anyone who is successful. The basic factor is enjoyment. It is vital to have that."

My own personal favourite definition of success is that it is a choice, a decision: what do you want to be, to do and to have.

This is summed up by the quote from the singer/songwriter, Joan Baez:

"You don't get to choose how you're going to die. Or when. You can only decide how you are going to live. Now!"

A great story that sums this up is related by the famous Kenyan long-distance athlete, Kip Keino. He once approached his American coach, a guy called Lou Tice, and they discussed their preparations for the upcoming 10,000 metres World Championships.

They discussed race tactics and the coach suggested that Keino, upon hearing the bell to signal the 25th and final lap, should attack hard and run this lap faster than any of the previous 24. Keino didn't agree and explained that it was at this stage when his lungs burnt and that his legs felt sore and his heart raced furiously that it was an impossible request from his coach. Tice stopped and thought. Eventually he asked Keino why he chose to run and compete. Keino explained the great pride he felt in knowing that the whole continent of Africa, along with his country, his village and his family would be watching him compete on the highest stage of all.

Tice listened intently and then said that he had thought about it and revised the tactics. When hearing that final lap bell, he told the athlete that he should sit on the kerb and that if he did this for a few seconds, his lungs, legs and heart would soon feel a lot better and then he could continue to run.

Keino blinked in disbelief at this advice and said *"but if I do that, I won't win the race!"*

The coach nodded and said: *"Exactly. You can choose to run and you can choose whether you are going to give your best or not"*.

An American sociologist, Dr Anthony Campolo, did some research where a group of elderly people, all of whom were aged 95 or over, were asked the following question: 'If you were to live your life over again, what would you do differently next time?'

According to Dr Campolo, the three top answers were summarised as follows:

1. Have less regrets.

It seems that this was related more to what people didn't do as opposed to what they did do in their lives.

2. Take time out to reflect more.

Some people felt that they just drifted along with the crowd and spent little, if any time, considering what they really wanted from life. Think about this, though. If you have read up to this point of the book and thought about the questions posed within it, you are not one of these people are you? You have taken the time to reflect and should congratulate yourself.

3. Leave a legacy.

People wanted to feel that their lives on earth had counted for something and that in some way, their life would be remembered after they had gone. In other words, they wanted the people at their funeral to know what their purpose was, what they stood for.

Most people will go to the time and effort of writing a will at some stage of their lives to say what they want to happen after they die. Fewer people put the same effort and attention into what they want to happen whilst they are alive. You have the chance to start now.

Sir John Jones, the headmaster of the UK's worst school, who transformed it into the most improved school within 7 years, said that 85% of us will go to the grave having only used a maximum of 15% of our potential.

You have a choice whether you want to remain amongst that 85%.

Action:

Think about what is most important to you and what you most enjoy doing. What makes you happy? Ask the people you care about, what success means to them. The more time you spend thinking about what success means to you, the more likely it will happen.

Consider what success means to you, in relation to your career (paid or unpaid work), your relationships and to your recreation time.

Take some time to sit down and think about what success means to you. Write down what success would look, feel and sound like for you in your life both now and in five years time.

Some questions which will help you answer this are:

• Write a list of things that you do not like to do. Make the list as long as you like.

• Write a list of things that you do like to do. Make the list as long as you like.

• When does time seem to fly? What do you do, at work or play, that makes time appear to fly? Write a list of those things. Make the list as long as you like.

• Think about what energises you? Which things make you feel better after you have completed them, than you felt before you started? Make a list of all those things. Make it as long as you like.

• Think about the things you are good at? Include things you do at work at play. Write a list of the things you are good at. Make it as long as you like.

Now look at the list of things you are good at and cross out any that you may do well, but do not energise you, that you leave to the end of the day, or that make time drag.

Now you should have a clearer idea which of these elements you may want to include in your life, to help you become a success.

Liquid goal-d

"If you are going to be having goals, you might as well make them big ones!"

Donald Trump

In the 1950's, there was a study carried out at Harvard University where the students were questioned about who had goals. Not surprisingly, virtually everyone said that they did. They were then asked how many had actually put these goals into writing and the answer to this question was only 3% of the group.

This study was followed up 30 years later and the 3% that had written down their goals were worth more than the other 97% combined.

Amazing or just a coincidence?

That's up to you to decide but as long as your goals only stay inside your head, you run the risk of them only ever being dreams. Remember, we highlighted in the last chapter that success is a choice which you can make. You can't necessarily have everything you want but you can have anything you want and the choice you face is what do you want to be, to do and to have. You have to make some decisions about how you are going to spend your time and where you are going to put your energies, otherwise one day you'll wake up at 100 years old and be answering questions about your biggest regrets in life.

When you think about your goals, ask yourself whether you are a hen or a pig? In the ham and egg story, the hen is merely involved but the pig is committed.

SMART RAS

This isn't a spelling mistake. Let me explain.

Having a written goal is likely to get you into that top 3% of the population. If, however, you are going to go to the trouble of writing down a goal, I would suggest that you copy the examples of many successful people, such as the golfer Greg Norman, who writes his goals by using the SMARTS method:

"Setting goals for your game is an art. The trick is in setting them at the right level, neither too low nor too high."

Imagine that you have a goal to lose some weight. It's pretty vague isn't it? Instead, make your goals:

Specific

Define exactly what you want to accomplish and focus on only one thing.

Example: "I want a lose two stones in weight by March 2006."

Measurable

Use percentages, cost, quality, numbers, it doesn't matter what, but you should think of all of the ways you can measure your progress in order to be able to say whether you 'did' or 'didn't' achieve it.

Example: giving it a clear measure of weight you want to lose (2 stones) and a time measure (by March 2006) is a great example.

Achievable and Realistic.

Think of something that is within reach but which would still require you stretch to achieve it.

Example: Is two stones a realistic amount of weight to lose or are you kidding yourself?

This is your decision alone, as what may be achievable and realistic for you may not be for another. For example, your goal might be to run the London Marathon in 4 hours. For Paula Radcliffe, this would be a gentle jog.

If that voice in your head is telling you, as you write it, that you won't do it, the likelihood is that you won't. When you write the goal, write it as though you have already achieved it, in the present tense and use your senses to describe it. For example:

"I feel and look great now that I have lost weight."

Why should you do this? Well every time you read it (because you should put it somewhere like by your bed or on the fridge, where you will see it every day) your unconscious mind, your emotions and your RAS (more of which later) will kick in and support you in getting there.

Timed

Set yourself a deadline of when you will achieve your goal by. Be careful not to limit yourself by setting a goal which is too far in the future but, at the same time, a goal that it is too close can cause you to become demotivated instead and so, it's a question of finding the right balance.

Example: March 2006. Is six months a realistic time scale? It's not too far in the future that you can't imagine it yet its not too near to be unrealistic.

Step

The last step. What hard evidence will you need to prove to yourself that you have fulfilled your goal, that you have 'done' it? If your goal is about buying a house, it might be the moment when you put the key in the lock or it may be the minute you see the SOLD sign being taken down.

Karen Darke, who was paralysed at 21 after a climbing accident and who then achieved her dream of cycling across the Himalayas, explained that her 'step' was the moment when she watched the sun setting from the top of a mountain which she had just spent the previous couple of hours cycling up. Mark Holden, from North West Liquids, described his 'step' as imagining himself enjoying a beer with his fiancé after completing the London Marathon.

If you don't take the care to write down what you will see, hear, smell, touch and feel at this moment, you may fall short before you achieve your goal.

Example: you may imagine yourself standing in front a full length mirror in your bedroom trying on a new pair of jeans that you really wanted.

"Many of life's failures are people who did not realise how close they were to success when they gave up"

This was said by Thomas Edison, the inventor described by his teachers as a "blockhead", who carried out over 10,000 experiments, using over 3000 different types of material, including coconut hair, fishing line and bamboo before he found success with the light bulb and was able to light the world! Do you think that his 'step' was seeing a light bulb above his head?

Let's talk about your RAS. I'm not being rude here. Read on.

You will find that if you do take the time to think about and write down what your SMART goal is, 80% of the 'how' you achieve it will take care of itself. Bear with me while I explain why writing down your SMART goal will ensure that:

"a whole stream of events...unforeseen incidents and meetings...which no man could have dreamt will come your way" *(Goethe, a German doctor, military man and inventor.)*

It is down to, would you believe it, your RAS, which stands for Reticular Activating System (RAS), a small part of your brain, which is critical in helping you achieve your goals.

Let me illustrate what I mean.

When you drive through Port Sunlight on your way to work, how often do you notice the small details of your journey? Do you notice if they have painted the door of No. 29 green instead of red? Do you notice that the daffodils outside of No. 10 are now in bloom? Do you spot that the curtains in No. 45 are blue? Thought not. This is because our brains are receiving about 2 million pieces of data a second. If we were able to process all of this information, our brains would, quite literally, explode. And so we are only consciously aware of a few pieces of information at any one time.

Okay, so imagine you're driving through Tesco's car park, looking for a parking space. Suddenly you start to become aware of people carrying shopping bags and walking slowly, reverse lights on cars coming on and all sorts of other details which you would normally miss because you now need a parking space. This is your RAS working for you.

Stop for a second and think about your left foot and whether it is comfortable inside your shoe. Where was that thought until I just brought it to your attention? The answer is nowhere. You were looking after it on an unconscious level until I kicked your RAS into action.

Here's one last example of your RAS. Have you ever had a goal to own a particular type of car, let's say a yellow VW beetle. Once you have decided what car you want, have you ever noticed how you suddenly start to see loads of them on the roads, whereas before you hadn't? It is not that these cars weren't previously there, it just that you weren't consciously aware of them before.

It's the same when you set yourself a goal that you really want. Suddenly, you will find all sorts of coincidences and opportunities coming your way, which will help and support you in achieving your goal. Once I had decided that I wanted to write this book, I started to find ideas and quotes to use in it everywhere I looked, from the newspapers, television and conversations with people. One of the quotes I found was from the former US president, Abraham Lincoln, and I think that it neatly wraps up this chapter:

"When you know what you want to achieve, what your goal is, you will start to find yourself unconsciously keeping away from people and circumstances which continually knock what you are trying to achieve. It is small people who do that. You will also, unconsciously seek out and find yourself in the company of great people, who will support you and help you to recognise opportunities where there were previously none."

See, it does pay, therefore, to be a SMART RAS.

Action:

There are 2 basic parts of goal setting, which include taking small steps and then writing your goals in the SMARTS format.

It will be most useful for you to start thinking about small steps and then move on to writing them SMARTS.

PART A

SMALL STEPS:
The useful and easy way to start setting our goals is to get rid of our own tolerations (things we feel we should be doing but for whatever reasons we are not doing them).

STEP 1:
Define all your 'shoulds'.
Example: I should lose some weight.

STEP 2:
Explore reasons for your 'shoulds'.
Example: Because I don't feel confident about myself. Because it is not healthy to be overweight, etc.

STEP 3:
Change 'should' to want.
Example: I want to lose some weight.

STEP 4:
Make your 'want' positive.
Example: I want to be slimmer!

PART B

Now make your 'want' SMARTS.

SPECIFIC

MEASURABLE

ACHIEVABLE

REALISTIC

TIMED

'STEP'

Example: It is March 2006 and I have lost 2 stones in weight and I am 12 stones. I am standing in front of the mirror in m bedroom wearing a new shirt and jeans and I feel fitter, healthier and great.

Now, follow these steps and write your goal below:

Liquid thinkers

Mark Holden is a line operator in North West Liquids.

I am the manager of a local Sunday football team, which is something I've done for the last few years, ever since I injured my knee. One week, one of the lads from the team had been talking in the dressing room about his plans to do the London Marathon and it started to get me thinking.

Doing a marathon, especially the London Marathon, was one of those things that had always been bubbling away in the back of my mind, something I'd get round to doing, one day. I had never thought about it any specific terms. It had always seemed like a difficult but achievable challenge and so, I decided to give my old manager a call, as I knew that he had done it a couple of times before. At this stage, I only wanted to know a little bit more about it but once we started chatting and he told me about how fantastic the feeling of actually taking part and finishing it was, I knew there and then that I would do it.

If you had stopped me and asked me what sort of picture I had in my mind, when I thought about the marathon, it was probably the sort of image which you see on the telly: the finishing line, next to Buckingham Palace; loads of people cheering and going mad, that sort of thing. I imagined myself running, at full speed, along there and through the line. I suppose, it was this sort of picture in my head, which got me feeling excited about doing it. I hadn't given any thought about the hard work which would be involved at this stage.

I have got a bit of a reputation amongst my mates and my family of being a 'fly-by-night' sort of person. You know, the sort of fella who loses interest in things dead quickly. Let me give you an example. When I moved into our new house, over a year ago, I did just enough work to get comfy in it and I have been managing to put off doing the other jobs, which need doing. I'm not lazy. It's because the house is just comfortable enough.

So, when I told my missus what I was planning to do, she didn't really think that I was serious at first. We enjoy a good social life and we like going out quite a lot and so she thought that there was no way I wanted to do the marathon enough to cut down on the socialising to give the training my full commitment.

Liquid thinkers

This time, I knew differently and I started from the fact that I knew I was going to finish the marathon, one way or another. I then worked backwards from there. I started to think about how I could plan my training and preparation. I knew that I needed to tone down the ale and start eating better, as this would help my energy levels. I decided that I could make better use of my days off and so, I set myself some small targets, such as 'If I do cut the lawn in the morning, I will play golf in the afternoon' and that sort of thing. Being able to set goals like this, made it easier for me to plan and to make time to get out and train.

I did involve others and had a training partner, who was a mate from work who was also doing it, but most of the time, I would go out on my own. My routine was to do a day 'on' and a day 'off'

and gradually I built up, so that I was running between 8 and 15 miles along the Wirral peninsula pretty regularly.

I really started to enjoy the feeling of being able to run further than I thought I could and I liked the fact that I could feel myself improving and getting better the more I did it. I won't lie, I'll admit that there were some days when the weather was terrible and I just didn't fancy going out and running, but I would tempt myself with that image of myself crossing the finish line in London and imagine the feelings of achievement, which I knew I would enjoy when I did complete it and this would make me go out. If I hadn't have been prepared to do this, I would've felt a bigger failure if I had given-up and pulled out before even attempting it, than if I had somehow failed to finish on the day.

In the days and weeks beforehand, I spoke to loads of people that I knew had completed a marathon and I wasn't afraid to ask questions about how they had prepared and about how it felt to succeed. This was a big help; knowing that plenty of other people had been there and done it before, gave me a confidence boost and everyone was really encouraging. They were all happy to share little tips and bits of advice.

On the day itself, it was boiling hot and there wasn't a lot of wind about, which made it feel even more humid. Not ideal conditions to then go and run 26.1 miles. The atmosphere though was amazing and I was surprised how much this really helped to keep me going. Little kids would hold out their hands for you to 'high five' as you ran past and people came out of the pubs along the route to cheer and shout encouragement. By the end of the first half of the race, I was feeling good.

People had warned me about the stage in the race which all runners face, when you start to hurt and when doubts cave into your mind. I 'hit the wall' at 14 miles. This was the time when I really did start to doubt whether I could carry on.

I knew though, that it was a mental battle and I started to tell myself that I had run this distance in training loads of times before and that every pace I took, was a pace closer to finishing.
What helped was when I pictured myself running 5 miles in training and this allowed me to keep telling myself that I could do it. The crowd were also a massive help as they continued to shout encouragement. Slowly and gradually, I started to feel better and managed to keep going.

The feeling that I experienced when I did run past Buckingham Palace and crossed the finish line was absolutely amazing and was even better than I had imagined it would be, when I had first pictured that very same image, in my mind.

I had started out with a target of running it in around 4 hours and even though I came in just outside of this time, the sense of elation and satisfaction was overwhelming.

Would I do it again? Definitely. I am currently trying to persuade my fiancée, as we get married 5 days after next year's marathon!

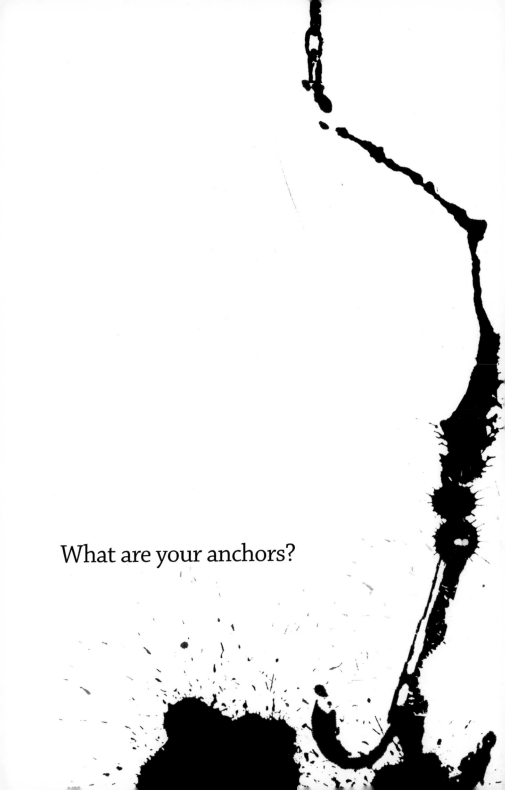

What are your anchors?

"The biggest problem with most people of today is that they don't stand for anything. Values provide directions. If you don't stand for something, you fall for everything."

Don Shula, head coach of Miami Dolphins.

What are your anchors? What do I mean by that, you ask. Think of the values, the mood, the emotions and the states which you mostly enjoy being in. What does it take to make you happy?

I have met a number of people that have gone through a health scare and afterwards have found peace within themselves. I have asked them what difference the scare has made to them and some of them have explained that it took the scare of nearly losing everything to make them realise just what was important to them.

Now without putting yourself through a near-death experience, take the time to stop and think about what in your life that is really valuable to you and to your ongoing happiness.

Once you know your values, you can construct your life's purpose and goals around them to ensure that when you reach your chosen destination and achieve your goals, you have done it in a way that will leave you feeling satisfied. Take the Canadian sprinter Ben Johnson. If his values were about truth and honesty, do you think that when he won the 100m gold medal in Seoul in 1988, he would have felt great, knowing that it had been done through the illegal use of steroids?

A great example of someone that met their goals without having to compromise their values was Muhammad Ali.

In 1967, during his first reign as world heavyweight champion, he was drafted into the US Army and ordered to go to Vietnam to fight. Despite the governments threats to strip him of the world title which he coveted and had worked so hard to achieve and the possibility of being thrown into prison for his refusal to be drafted, Ali knew his values, which included the belief that the war was wrong and he would not let himself be compromised (even when he was given the offer of being a figurehead for the army and of never having to face any conflict). He famously declared that: "I ain't got no quarrel with the Vietcong."

Instead, he accepted that he had to lose his title and wasn't able to fight again for over 3 years because his purpose, which was "to be the greatest" and his goal, which was to be the heavyweight champion of the world, would have felt hollow and worthless had he sacrificed his own values to achieve them.

Values are the rules which we construct our lives around. Nobody else can make you have particular values, they are unique to you, and you alone, as they are the rules which you will choose to live by and around which you will chase your version of success.

Think about your own values and think about how many of them are rules which are realistic and which are rules you can never hope to win by.

Let me give you an example. How many of you think that you would be really, truly happy and all your worries would be over if you came into a lot of money, like winning the lottery? I am sure you are aware that the odds on actually winning the lottery are about 14 million –to-one (or, my favourite way of explaining it is that you are more likely to go up to a stranger in a foreign country and guess their telephone number than win the lottery!) So why would you have this as a rule of making yourself truly happy? Wouldn't it better to follow the examples of those who have had health scares and tell us that they set rules for achieving happiness, such as being genuinely grateful to wake up in a morning, which are achievable for all of us.

Let me give you an idea about different things, which you might consider to be a value:

Success: do you want to be successful? Do you want to be the best in your chosen field?

Passion: is that something that you are excited about? Do you want to experience huge passion in everything you do and so will go the extra mile and do whatever it takes to feel it?

Fun: do you have fun as one of your values? Do you want to enjoy life to the full?

Greed: It was Michael Douglas's character, Gordon Gecko, in the film 'Wall Street', who said "greed is good" but you could choose this as one of your values if you are the sort of person who just wants more, more, more.

Enthusiasm: are you the sort of person who leaps out of bed determined to squeeze the most of the day?

Power: is power important to you? Do you want people to look at you and see someone who brings power to a situation?

Love: to love other people and to be loved. How do you feel about love?

Integrity/honesty: do you believe that truth is high on your list of values? Do you believe in telling the truth even if there are consequences?

Recognition: you may wonder how you could have recognition as a value, but some people do, because it plays an important part in their lives.

Control: is this a value for you? Do you want to be in control? Do you want to know exactly what's happening every minute of the day? Is control important to you and you are really clear about where you want to go? Are you a hands-on type of person?

Blame: do you find yourself blaming others for situations that occur around you? Do you want to know who is causing the problems so you can 'get to the bottom of it'?

Excitement: are you the type of person who loves bungee-jumping, jumping off cliffs or take risks? Do you think that excitement is within the business and about the work that you do? Do you think that excitement is within relationships? Could it be one of your values?

Security: do you want to be secure? do you want to know exactly where everything is going to be on a regular basis? Do you get home and love to know that certain things are going to be in a certain place? Do you like the feeling of total security?

Worry: do you find yourself worrying all the time? Believe that worrying is a way of showing that you care?

Contribution: do you believe that making a contribution is critical? Do you want to give your time and efforts to help others without any recognition? Are you the sort of person who is always the first volunteer?

Health: are you focused on your health? Do you carefully watch what you eat, believing that nourishment and vitality are the key to quality of life?

Creativity: do you look to be creative in all that you do? Are you constantly trying to think of new ways to do things? Do you think its important to think outside of the box and move the boundaries?

Even Homer Simpson knows what his values are:

"There is a an empty spot I've always had inside me. I tried to fill it with family, religion, community service but those were dead ends. I think that this chair and a beer is the answer."

Action:

Consider the values that were held by your parents, mentors and teachers. Write a list of them.

Take a look at the values you wrote down, and consider which of those you feel you should share, and those you actually do share.

Think about the times when you truly felt successful, when you surprised yourself how well you did.
Write a list of these times.

Now take a look at the list on the left. Can you think of a value, something you believe in, that helped inspire that success? For example, maybe you won a running race against all odds? The value that led you may have been 'practice' or 'self-belief' or 'hard work' or 'education' or 'teamwork'.

Go back to the chapter where you wrote about what success means to you? Do you begin to see your values emerging?

What are the five most important values in your life and work? What are the rules and conditions which will allow you to live your life and make decisions which fit within your own personal rule book?

1.

2.

3.

4.

5.

Future reflections

"*The man who has no imagination, has no wings*".

Muhammad Ali, 1963

Let's return to the example of Muhammad Ali, the most famous sportsman in history, as it was Ali who coined the phrase 'future history' and it is Ali who offers the best example of what it means. When he first burst onto the world boxing scene, he was the first sportsman who started to make bold predictions about which round he was going to win in. He would confidently declare his chosen route of victory in poetry, like:

"This boy likes to mix, so he'll fall in 6!"

and he went on to make these sort of predictions in 19 of his 61 fights.

How many times do you think that he was accurate with the predictions of the round he won in?

The actual answer is 17.

In 1963, before he became the heavyweight champion, he fought Archie Moore, a well-respected former champion and many people viewed it as the first real test of the young Ali's career. At the press conference, Ali looked at the huge, imposing giant he was going to face and said:

"Don't block the aisles, don't block the door. You will all go home, when Archie goes in four!"

Archie Moore, a man who brought many years of ring craft and experience, couldn't believe the audacity of this cocky kid. He thought that Ali was crazy and just laughed.

After the press conference, Ali went back to his hotel room, lay down and relaxed from his head to his toes and he started to use his imagination.

In his mind, he saw the press conference just as it had been. He saw himself making that prediction but then he started to visualise the days and the weeks ahead and saw himself building up the fight. He saw himself doing amazing things in training: imagining himself preparing and getting stronger and better than Moore. He knew that if Moore was up at 5.00am to do his road work, he'd be up at 4.00am. He envisioned himself during his sparring sessions, getting bigger and stronger.

He then imagined the day of the fight and imagined himself arriving outside the stadium and getting out of the car, hearing the crowd chant only one name. He could hear it over and over again: 'Ali, Ali...' He would intensify the image; increase the feeling, bringing it closer to him, imagining and feeling every single word, every single emotion that went with it.

Then he pictured himself going into the dressing room and imagined the feeling of the bandages being wrapped on his hands, feeling the gloves being laced on and he saw himself standing strong. He heard them announce his name as he walked into the arena. In his own mind, he sensed the crowd going crazy, screaming for him. Only his name was screamed; everybody was on his side.

In his vision, he saw himself getting into the ring and looking across the crowd. He could see every single person screaming his name and he could hear it over and over again, intensifying, increasing in volume, increasing in emotion: 'Ali, Ali...' Then he turned to face Moore and saw him shrink small. He touched gloves and started to fight.

He would visualise each round – mentally rehearsing the outcome he wanted. He saw them exactly as he had planned it. Connecting, brilliant blows, doing the famous Ali shuffle, floating like a butterfly, stinging like a bee!

He saw the first three rounds in perfect focus. And then, as the bell signalled the start of the fourth round, he moved out purposefully into the ring's centre. He waited, patiently until the right moment. Boom! He connected with Moore and saw him go down. When he fell, Ali imagined himself standing over him and the referee making the count – 'one, two, three...' At the point, when he knew he had won, he would freeze-frame the image and surround it in brilliant white light. This image was his 'future history.'

By the way, he did go on to win in the 4th round.

Was this luck or just plain talent? Well, neither exactly.

How about this as a further example of the power of 'future history'? At the American University, UCLA in California, the coach divided his basketball team into three groups. He got every player to throw 100 shots and then measured how many each group had scored in total. He then gave each group different sorts of practise. One group did nothing; the next group stayed on court and practised 'shooting hoops', where the players take a free throw at the basket, and the third group went back to the dressing room and were made to sit quietly and just picture themselves shooting hoops and imagining how the ball would feel in their hands, the sound of the ball rattling through the basket and the emotions that they would feel when

it went through. The three groups did the same activity for a month. The coach brought all of the groups back onto court and had a competition to see which one would score the most consecutive points. Guess who won? You've got it. The team who had done the visualisation exercise consistently won. To check that it wasn't a fluke, he tried it for a further month and, guess what? The group that had continued the mental rehearsal won even by an even higher score.

Still need convincing?

How about this one then? Psychologists in England have devised a mental training system that can increase your golf putting skills by 50% in 6 weeks. A group of amateur golfers were given a choice of either watching a video of themselves or they could listen to an audio tape of their putts being holed for 10 minutes a day. They were not allowed to actually go onto a course and physically practise any putts but they could recreate the movement in their heads only. At the end of the 6 weeks, both groups improved massively. The group using video increased their putting skills by 57% and the group using audio tapes increased by 47%. No-one had actually picked up a club during that period! It was purely down to the power of the mind being able to conjure up images of success.

Convinced yet? Well you should be, as by using the same, simple techniques and methods of clearly picturing and visualising what you want, your chances of success start to dramatically improve.

Action:

Here is a brilliant exercise that is worth trying with a mate or your partner. Find a quiet place and ask your partner to sit and listen to you. It isn't a conversation as you will be doing most of the talking but imagine that it is two years ahead in time and you are looking back at the last two years.

Now start to answer the following questions (remember to use past tenses such as 'I have' or 'I did'):

Where have you been on holiday? Was it good? What did you do? Who did you go with?

Where are you working? What has work been like? Are you still doing the same job?

Where are you living? Describe your house. Who are you living with? (Take care in answering this question if you are with a partner!)

What have you achieved in the last couple of years that you are most proud of and why?

Now think back to the last time you did that. When was it?

If you are like most of us, the answer is probably never. So why bother to do it?

Generally when we talk about what we are going to do, it tends to be at some unspecified point in the future ("one day I'm going to...) and it tends to focus on the action itself ("...I'll paint the fence!") whereas, when you look at your 'future history', this is an exercise which is all about what has been done and, most significantly, it engages your emotions, as it focuses on what you have done and what you have already achieved. If you can't get excited about your achievements, who will?

When you did the exercise, did you quickly find yourself running out of things to say? That isn't a problem. It just indicates that you haven't spent enough time in the future yet. Keep practising, it will become easier with habit. Charles Kettering, an inventor and a business consultant, said:

"My interests are in the future, because I'm going to spend the rest of my life there!"

Practise spending your time thinking about your future, until it becomes easier to make the images appear clearly in your mind. It is something you can do at any time, such as when you're driving to work or just before you go to sleep.

Which brings me neatly on to my next point. You may know what you want to happen in your future history but the images may not still come through clearly. Again, don't worry about it. Trust me, it will come with repeated practise. For example, Robin Reid, the 1992 Olympic boxing medallist tells of how he and his fellow Olympic athletes repeated this exercise. They didn't sort of, kind-of-like, see themselves, you know, sort of winning the race or the event. They saw it in microscopic, minute detail. And they rehearsed it over and over until they could hold it perfectly and could play it back repeatedly, like a DVD.

By spending this time thinking about your future, it is also a great opportunity to find out what not to do. If you find yourself failing to get excited by an idea that you have always thought you wanted to do, maybe there is a lesson there? Lots of people say that they have always wanted to run a marathon. You may be one of them. However, when you were talking about it, did you not find yourself imagining the moment when you cross the finish line after 26.1 miles and feel your heart beat a little quicker with excitement? Instead, did it make you feel only dread? Now, it may be that you need to practise your ability to see your 'future history'. If you constantly have this same feeling of dread, then maybe this isn't the goal for you. If you don't have the energy or enthusiasm to make it happen, forget it! Use your energy for another goal that does make your spine tingle.

Action:

Clarence Day, the former US president, said about his own goals:

"You can't sweep people off their feet if you can't be swept off your own."

As I have mentioned, you must repeat this exercise as often as possible because the technique works by strengthening the mental pathways in your brain which are involved in making the action happen. It is like walking across a field. The first time you do it, you will leave only a faint pathway of where you have trodden but if you walked along that same pathway 2/3 times a day, the stronger and more clear the pathway becomes.

After the Rugby World Cup Final in 2003, Johnny Wilkinson was asked whether he was nervous when receiving the ball, to execute his last second winning drop goal. His response:

"No. I've been here a million times before."

He also used the same techniques, of future reflecting and imagining success constantly, before he actually did it.

Go back to your SMART goal and start to make and run your own movies in your mind. Imagine yourself successfully achieving your goals and then do your best to think about it in really clear, precise detail as often as possible.

You can repeat this exercise whenever and wherever you want. The more you do it, the more likely it is to happen.

"When your will comes into conflict with your imagination, your imagination will always carry the day."
Emile Coue

Liquid thinkers

Brian Higginson is a Safety Leader in North West Liquids.

In December 1997, my wife, Christine, had noticed a lump which had developed in her breast and she went to Clatterbridge Hospital to get it checked out. The doctors did what is known as a 'fine needle aspiration', followed by a biopsy and when the results came back, the news was good. She was given the all clear.

Christine, however, wasn't entirely convinced and in April 1998 she was still worried as she noticed that the lump had begun to change shape. She returned to the hospital and had the lump surgically removed. After the operation, the doctors did some analysis but assured Christine that they were "99.9% certain everything would be fine."

We waited for the results to come back...

That June was the summer when England were playing in the World Cup finals in France. Christine and I had saved up some money to go to the USA with the kids and were planning to visit Universal studios, Disneyland and all of the other sights. After the normal, early years of struggling to bring up young kids (we had two sons, Alec who, at the time, was 14 years old and George, 12), everything was beginning to look rosy.

Also, at this time I was studying for my NEBOSH certificate, along with Richie Clarke (No 4). This meant that I had to go away for a two week course which involved studying at the Grosvenor Hotel in Stratford upon Avon. During the first week, I'd been keeping in touch with Christine everyday chatting and checking about the usual stuff ("How are you? How are the kids, etc?")

On the first Thursday of the course, I nipped up to my hotel room during the lunch break to ring home. I knew that Christine had had an appointment in the morning at the hospital and so I obviously wanted to see what the news was. I didn't get an answer. At the time, I thought that it was a bit odd as I would have expected her to be back. I rang again at the end of the day, which was about 4:30pm and still got no reply. When I rang again at about 6 o'clock I finally got through. Christine answered the phone and sounded a little subdued.

"I've got it", she quietly told me, "I've got cancer".

I felt myself go numb. I was shocked, to say the least. In fact, I'd go even further... I was absolutely devastated. As the words started to sink in, I became very upset.

Liquid thinkers

"I'm coming home", I told her but Christine would have none of it. She told me, in no uncertain terms:

"Don't you start whinging. I've got the problem and I will deal with it"

That evening, I just didn't know what to say or do.

The lecturer had arranged a curry evening, followed by a walk into town with the other delegates and the enjoyment of a few drinks. I felt empty and gutted but forced myself along to the restaurant, where I pushed the food around my plate, quickly made my excuses and left. This evening, one of the first thoughts that entered my head and remained was:

"if I lose Christine, how will I cope with the kids?"

Talk about selfish!

The other delegates came and met me in the bar after they'd finished their meal. They could sense that there was something wrong and so I told them the news which had cast a shadow over the whole evening. In those circumstances what can anybody say? The lecturer advised me to give up on the course and get myself home and Richie immediately offered to drive me back to the Wirral. When I look back now, though and think about it, I realise that the telephone conversation I had with Christine was just the beginning of her fight with the "Big C". I told Richie and the others what Christine had said:

"There's no point coming home tonight; I'll see you tomorrow."

When I got home on the Friday, I spent the weekend with Christine and we sat and discussed what was going to happen next. She was to have an operation the following Friday and she was very positive that she would get through this thing.

"Don't give up on the course. Go back, take your exams and pass!" she encouraged me.

On the Thursday, she went to the hospital to prepare for the following days operation. On the morning of the procedure, a nurse came to see her and began to explain that the registrar wanted to have a word with her. The registrar carefully explained the surgery was available in these circumstances. She could opt for either:

a lumpectomy i.e. removal of the tumour from the breast with a small amount of surrounding tissue or:

a mastectomy, which is the removal of all or part of the breast, sometimes removing surrounding muscles and lymph nodes.

Christine was dumbfounded when the registrar asked her what she would prefer.

"Just get rid of the lot" she told him.

I got home from Stratford upon Avon that evening and went up to the hospital. When I arrived on the ward, the nurse pointed to where I would find Christine. She was fast asleep and looked so peaceful, I just didn't have the courage to wake her. In fact, I just wanted to run away from the place. I turned and told the nurse that she was asleep and I would have left it at that and gone back home. The nurse turned me around and told me to wake her up. I quietly called to Christine and when she awoke, she smiled. After what she'd been through, I couldn't believe how she could find it within herself do that!

With cancer, things have to get worse before they can start to get better. After the operation, Christine went to see the consultant to discuss what further treatment was necessary. He told her that she required six months of chemotherapy and radiotherapy. During this visit, he also told her that it was worse than they had initially thought. Christine was diagnosed as having second stage cancer and that the cancer cells had also been found in her lymph nodes, which were also removed during the operation. We had gone from being 99.9% certain that there was no problem to this diagnosis.

This was the beginning of the long haul.

At first, it seemed that Christine was alright. She'd go along to the hospital and they'd put the tubes in and then administer the chemo'. However, as time wore on you could start to see the toll it was beginning to take on her. She was becoming increasingly weary and nauseous. The chemo' really knocked the stuffing out of her but she was so determined to beat this thing.

A couple of years later, she told me about a radio programme which she had listened to about a person, who was also suffering with cancer, and about how that person had focused upon the effected part of their body and "thought it out". Christine told me that she had literally lay in bed, in the dark and thought about exactly where the cancer was and she willed it to disappear.

To have to endure chemotherapy is bad enough, at the best of times, but to have six months worth and I could see Christine starting to fade away before my eyes. We have a photograph that was taken at New Year and, although she never completely lost her hair, you can see that it had thinned out and she looked really gaunt. It never stopped her though. She used to say that she was a mum and she wouldn't let this thing interfere with her being a mum!

After being poisoned for six months, because that's exactly what chemotherapy does to you, Christine was prescribed an anti-cancer drug (tamoxifen) which she would have to take for the next five years. The problem

Liquid thinkers

for women who suffer from cancer at this stage in their life (at the time, she was 44 years of age) are all of the 'extras' that you get from the chemotherapy. There's no way that you want the 'extras' but you don't have any choice and get them anyway! As if having cancer isn't bad enough, in the first place, she then had to cope with the onslaught of the menopause... and I mean onslaught!

The sensation that she got from this is tantamount to having her insides burning her up... and there's more! Apart from the anti-cancer drug that she had to take, she also has to take daily, for the rest of her life, calcium supplements because the chemo' gives you a nice little helping of osteoporosis.

At first, Christine would meet with a consultant and he'd check her out every three months after her treatment. When

she asked him if there was anything that she could take to help her with the menopause, the consultant said:

"Sorry but no. HRT can't be administered to you because of the cancer and so I suggest, to combat osteoporosis, you take plenty of load-bearing exercise, such as power walking!"

What has happened since?

After five years, Christine was taken off the tamoxifen. The consultant still sees her on an annual basis and he will keep doing so for the next five years, due to her having cancer at a young age but the whole cancer experience has had a dramatic effect on Christine's life.

Her job, at the time she was diagnosed, was working as a care assistant in an old peoples' home. She really loved the job and even in her spare time, she would

take the residents, who were wheelchair bound, out for walks. Because of what had happened, she couldn't carry on in that line of work any longer. The holiday to the USA, which we had so looked forward to, was put on hold for twelve months. Another love of her life is gardening, and with the removal of the lymph nodes, any scratches on her arms and it swells like a balloon.

Has it stopped her doing what she wanted to do?

Not at all. After some hassle from insurance companies about her condition, we finally managed to get the kids to America and we travelled along the west coast - from Las Vegas to San Francisco – where we did helicopter rides, visited the Grand Canyon; the works!

We've also spent three weeks in Vietnam, staying, at first, in Ho Chi Minh city; travelled for three days down the Mekong Delta where we crawled through the Cu Chi tunnels. There were six of us in the party which went down into the tunnels and the only one who made it the full distance, in the sweltering heat, at least 25ft below ground, was Christine.

We've been back to the States on a 'city slicker'- type holiday in the mid west - riding horseback, herding cattle; white water rafting on the Shoshone river.

Next year, she's planned for us to go to South America for three weeks Brazil, Uruguay and Argentina.

She still continues to potter about in the garden, even though, occasionally, when she gets a scratch, she has one arm that looks like Gandhi's whilst the other one looks like Arnold Schwarzenegger's.

She also manages to often get away on field trips with the local history group and if you ever are walking in the fields at Storeton, you'll see Christine power-walking, like a demon.

There is, however, one story that captures just what effect the cancer has had on our lives.

One of the big milestones for us was Christine's 50th birthday. She loves to drive and she'd never had a new car. I was determined that we should put this right. We went and had a look at some of the cars on the Vauxhall parking lot and she was eyeing up a Corsa.

"Do you really want that one though, Christine?" I asked her.

She told me 'yes', but I wasn't convinced. "What would you really like?"

She thought about it and then said that the one she'd really like was the Astra Convertible, which was in the corner of the lot.

"That's it then. Let's get it!", I told her.

You'll see her occasionally for two weeks of the year driving her car with "the lid off" (English weather see!).

Life altering experiences are all well and good, but the only piece of advice I'd give you is don't wait for something drastic to come along and wake you up. Christine's attitude is:

"Seize the moment. Life's too short to be hanging around waiting for things to happen"

What's next, I often wonder. If she could, it'd probably be a trip to the moon.

As Confucius says...If you shoot for the stars and hit the moon, it's OK. But you've got to shoot for something. A lot of people don't even shoot.

Turn water into wine

"Within you right now is the power to do things you never dreamed possible. this power becomes available to you as soon as you change your beliefs."

Maxwell Maltz

Did you know that a flea can jump great heights? In fact, they can jump the equivalent height of a human jumping a house. If you have a dog that has ever had fleas, that fact shouldn't come as a great surprise to you. If you ever do catch a flea, here is a brilliant experiment to try with it.

If you put a flea in a jar and then put a piece of cardboard on top of it, despite being able to jump far higher than the top of the jar, once the flea bangs its head against the card a few times, it will never again, in its whole life, jump higher than the height of the card on top of the jar. That way they are easy to control and you need never worry about them again. This is how they train the fleas in flea circuses.

What has this got to do with you and your beliefs you may be asking. Bare with me.

Once you have got rid of its fleas, here's an experiment for dogs that is interesting to note. In the 1960's Dr Martin Seligman of the University of Pennsylvania noticed during an experiment involving some dogs, that when they experienced any physical pain they just gave up and lay down, whimpering and staying in pain. He was fascinated by this and wanted to investigate further and so he carried out another stage to his investigations.

He put dogs into three groups, A, B and C. Dogs in group A were placed in a box and then given an electric shock. The dogs could stop the shock by pressing a bar with their nose and they learned to do this pretty quickly! Dogs in group B were placed in another box and were given a similar shock but they had no way of stopping it. Finally, dogs in group C were placed in the box but were not given any shocks at all.

The next day, the same dogs were placed in a different box, which had a low barrier placed down the middle of it. One side of the box gave off an electric shock when the dogs were placed next to it but, by stepping over the low barrier to the other side of the box, they could escape the electric shock.

Guess what happened?

The dogs in group A (those that had been able to turn the shock off, the day before) and group C dogs (those that hadn't got any shocks) very quickly learned to step over the barrier and escape the pain of the electric shock. Group B dogs (the ones that couldn't control the shocks in the first part of the experiment) didn't even try to escape. Instead, they just conceded immediately, lay down and whimpered. They believed that they had no control over events and just gave up right away.

Now the sceptics amongst you may say 'but they're dogs aren't they?' How many times, then, do you think that it takes humans to give up and succumb to similar levels of helplessness?

Dr Seligman wondered this, as well and so he tried a similar experiment where a group of volunteers were put into a room with 8 doors leading out of it. All of the doors were locked and then a deafening noise, like the sound of radio static, was played into the room. The volunteers all immediately scrambled to get out of the room but found the doors to be locked, and so sat back down again and put up with the horrible noise. Just as they all sat back down, Dr Seligman went round and unlocked all of the eight doors. Over the next three hours, how many people got back up and tried the doors again, to see if there was any escape from the horrible noise?

None of them. They had learned to be helpless after just one attempt.

The point of these experiments is that we all have beliefs, which then drive our actions and behaviours to produce certain results.

When we talk about identifying your purpose in life and the goals you want to achieve, it is the beliefs you hold that are the most important factor in achieving them. It is your own beliefs that will decide whether you will be successful. It is a simple formula: if you change the belief, you immediately change the behaviour and, therefore, you change the results which you will enjoy.

Henry Ford was the pioneer behind the first mass-produced motor car. He had a clear goal to make the car the mode of transport of the future and he had to overcome a lot of initial scepticism. He remained true to his own beliefs and didn't allow others to change them. He said:

"If I had listened to what my customers believed they wanted...I would have made a faster horse!"

It is an amazing admission but, it doesn't even matter if what you choose to believe is actually true or not. After all, you once believed that Father Christmas was real and your forefathers and ancestors once believed that the earth was flat, but if you do actually believe in something, at a deep, subconscious level, this is what will dictate how you behave, every minute of every day.

Talking of Father Christmas, think back to the time when you believed that he was a real person. Do you remember how it would affect your behaviour during December, when you believed that you wouldn't get any presents if you were badly behaved? It relates back to the formula:

Beliefs = behaviour = result.

In this case the 'result' was presents from Father Christmas.

It is how you behave, on a regular and consistent basis, that will decide the sort of results you get. The formula is really simple. If you change the beliefs at one end, you will change the results at the other.

As we go through our life, many of the barriers and obstacles that stop us from being successful come from within our own heads. We create and set limits for ourselves and then convince ourselves that it's impossible to go beyond those limits.

Once these barriers are proven to be breakable, we often look back and realise that the barrier was self imposed in our minds. It didn't actually exist in reality.

Homer Simpson understood this truth:

"Facts are meaningless. You could use facts to prove anything that is even remotely true."

Let me offer you, what I consider, to be the most powerful example of how beliefs can affect results. This was a belief that the whole of mankind held and had become accepted as fact over the centuries.

Since man had started to run and be measured against the clock, no-one had ever run a metric mile in under 4 minutes. On May 5th, 1954, the world record for this distance was 4 minutes and 1.4 seconds. To run it in under 4 minutes was a barrier that many "experts" felt was impossible to cross. In fact, the British Medical Council 'knew' that the human body couldn't run that fast.

The following day, a 25 year old medical student, called Roger Bannister, ran the distance in 3 minutes and 59.4 seconds; a fraction of a second below the impossible barrier. What is most amazing about his feat is the story which followed.

Within 46 days of Bannister breaking the record, a New Zealand athlete, John Landy, broke the record by running 3 minutes and 57.9 seconds. By the end of the year, two men – Bannister and Landy – had managed to break the 4 minute barrier in the same race. Astonishingly, by the end of 1957, just over two and half years after it had been proven to be a false belief, 16 runners had also gone on to prove it and beat the clock. The lid had been removed from the jar. By 1999, the world record for the distance had lowered 19 times and, to date, over 955 athletes have ran sub-four minute miles, accomplishing it on an amazing 4700+ times.

Think about yourself. What barriers are keeping you back?

Action:

Successful people have radically different beliefs to most of the population. These people know beliefs act as a powerful filters to how you experience the world. They understand that you don't believe what you see but rather you see what you believe. If you believe that the world is a bad place; you will probably find enough evidence to convince yourself that it is. The question is not, which is true, but which will serve you best in leading the life you want to lead.

Go back to your list of goals from the earlier chapter. Pick one of your goals. Now be as honest as possible and write down the obstacles which are stopping you achieving it. Next to them, indicate which reasons you believe are really impossible and which ones you could overcome with some thought and effort. Be brutal and challenge your own thinking. Share it with others and ask for their honest views on what is really impossible.

Some examples of barriers you may be imposing on yourself are:

Time	Debts
Money	Knowledge
Location	Qualifications
My boss	Being a woman
My partner	Being a man
Disability	Lack of transport
Being too fat	Fear of failure
Being too thin	Worrying about others
Lack of confidence	Illness
No support	Children
Laziness	Religion

Buy a book about one of your heroes and then compare your beliefs with those of successful people.

Notes:

Deckchairs on the Titanic

"If you wish to know your past life, look to your present circumstances. If you wish to know your future life, look to your present actions."

Buddhist saying

There are two factors which determine how we spend our time. There are the things that are classed as urgent ("I must do it and I must do it now!") and there are things that are classed as important, actions which contribute towards our goals. When you know this, you can start to allocate your time and activities into four main categories, which are:

Fire fighting (activities which are urgent and important)

Fire prevention (activities which are important)

False alarms (activities which are urgent)

Fire escapes (activities which are neither urgent nor important)

Let's look at each area in detail, as this will help you to plan your time better and help you achieve your goals, which you have identified.

Fire fighting

These are the times when you are reacting to the world around you, like when the phone is always ringing or when your boss is angry and demanding action or when the factory lines are always going down or when the kids are crying.

If this sounds familiar and you think that you are spending a lot of your time in this area, it is likely to be because you are not prioritising effectively.

By the way, if you have read the above and thought that this is your preferred style of operating, just ask yourself how many fires are you actually responding to and how many fires are you actually responsible for starting? Some of the best fire-fighters are also the best arsonists as they enjoy the feeling of always being active and available to help. The question is whether you are putting your energies into the right areas, which contribute to your own goals.

Fire prevention

The more time you spend in this area will mean the less time you will have to spend fighting fires and dealing with urgent and important issues. This is because you are planning, training, innovating and heading problems off before they become raging infernos. These issues don't depend on you getting involved and tackling them. You have to act first, to anticipate and solve them.

A great example of this is given in Sir Clive Woodward's book 'Winning!' He writes about the last seconds of England's World Cup win and he studies every pass, every move and every thought which the players took in those crucial, dying seconds of the 2003 Final. He was able to identify every area of innovation, practise and planning that he and his coaching team had taken, over the previous six years, in anticipation of that very moment when Johnny Wilkinson kicked the winning points.

He didn't wait until he was in the heat of the moment and decide to leave anything to chance. Instead, he had deliberately spent a large amount of his time in the 'fire prevention' box and had accounted for every possible eventuality, including the requirement of a last second winner!

One great example of fire prevention was Clive Woodward's introduction of a training method, which he called T-CUP (Total Control Under Pressure). This is a technique, which is taught to the elite soldiers of the SAS. Woodward had noticed that when the team had lost their previous 3 Grand Slam matches, the players had lost all composure and control when they were chasing the game and they had reverted to a style which wasn't their normal approach and which played straight into the hands of their opponents.

T-CUP training involved putting his players in pressurised situations and then teaching them how to handle their own emotions and not to panic. In convincing his players of the benefits of this coaching, he delivered a perfect example of prioritisation.

He explained this by starting from the players' goal, which was to win the World Cup. If they lost control, they would lose their discipline. If they lost their discipline, they would lose penalties. If they lost penalties, they would lose points. If they lost points, they would lose games. If they lost games, they would lose the world cup. When he explained it in these terms, the players all understood why they had to prioritise.

False alarms

This box is a deception and, although it feels like fire-fighting, it isn't. Events here feel as though they are urgent because of the noises of emergency and panic which people make. On closer inspection, you will find that it's usually a matter which is urgent only to them alone.

Fire escapes

This is the area where you find yourself doing anything, such as standing by the coffee machine, tidying the house or other easy distractions and excuses, which is like rearranging deckchairs whilst the Titanic sinks rather than doing what really needs to be done. Does this sound familiar to you?

Action:

LIFE PLANNING EXERCISE

Think about the 5 most important things in your life. For example, these may include your family; your parents; your career; your hobbies; your dreams, etc. Now grade them 1-10 on how happy you are with the amount of time you spend on them. (1= not happy; 10 = very happy).

Now think about what you would like the ratings to be. Grade them 1-10 on what you wish the time spent was.

This should give you a good indication on where you are spending most of your time. Is it in the areas and percentages which you want?

"The things that matter most never be at the mercy of things that matter least." Goethe.

Where do you spend most of your time? When you have your goals, make a list of all of the actions you can think of that it'll take to achieve it. Work back from your final outcome, figure out the main steps you need to take before you can achieve your goal and write them down (remember the 3% of Harvard graduates who wrote their goals?) Can you take just one small step a day based on your priorities?

	PRIORITY	CURRENT	REALITY
1.			
2.			
3.			
4.			
5.			

Swim with sharks or dolphins?

"Start each day with a smile and get it over with".

W.C. Fields

"There are men in your squad we wouldn't go into battle with" said the Royal Marine senior training instructor and rattled their names off.

"But why? What is it about them? They are clearly great at their jobs. Why wouldn't you go into battle with them?"

"It's not about their skills, Clive. It's about their attitude and their effect on the team. There are hundreds of soldiers who can run for three days, think on their feet and handle a weapon. But some aren't suited to working in a high-pressure team situation. It might be the smallest trait, like a moan when the going gets tough. One wrong team player can sap all the energy from a group."

This was a conversation between Clive Woodward and a Royal Marine trainer, after a team-building exercise, which Woodward had arranged, to discover who he should recruit to his team to go and win the World Cup. The Royal Marines trainer identified two groups of people in the team. Energisers and Energy Sappers.

The definitions for these terms include:

Energy Sappers – *verb. bleed, deplete, devitalise, drain, erode, exhaust, undermine, weaken, wear down. We will refer to them as probability thinkers.*

Energisers – *noun. drive, efficiency, exertion, fire, force, intensity, power, spirit, stamina, strength. We will refer to them as possibility thinkers.*

The thing is, not only do you become what you think about most of the time, but you also become like the people who you spend most of your time with.

Sir John Jones regularly speaks to newly qualified teachers and he cites one main difference, which makes teachers successful or not. It is not how well they know their subject or how well they can control a class. It is where they sit in the staff room.

He challenges them to think about whether they sit with people who love their job, enjoy the challenge of teaching and love the lifestyle it affords them or do they sit with those who love nothing more than to moan, gripe and bellyache about the job, the management, the canteen or the tea. These are the people who influence whether you are going to be a success or not. Sir John calls this second group, 'dream snatchers', the people who haven't achieved their dreams and will stop you achieving yours.

Robbie Williams wrote a song about one of these 'dream snatchers', which he included on his 'Life Thru a Lens' album. It was dedicated to one of his teachers who couldn't be bothered to learn his name for six years and who had laughed about his ambitions to be a pop star, suggesting, instead, that he join the army:

Hello Sir

Hello Sir, remember me?
I'm the man you thought I'd never be
The boy who you reduced to tears
Lad called 'thingy' for six whole years.
Yes, that's right, my name's Bob
The one who landed the pop star's job
The one you told, look don't touch
The kid who wouldn't amount to much.

Well, I'm here and you're still there
With a fake sports car and receding hair.
Dodgy Farah trousers that you think
are smart
Married to the woman who teaches art.

Married to the life, married to the school
I wanna sing and dance Sir; now who's
the fool?
Sing and dance, you thought I was barmy
Settle down thingy, join the army.

And who are you to tell me this?
The dream I want I'll have to miss
Sir is God, he's been given the right
To structure lives overnight.

Now I know life's true path
Tanks and guns that'll be a laugh
No, not me I'm a mega civilian
I won't lead my life riding pillion.

But thanks for the advice and I'm sure
it'll do
For the negative dickheads just like you.
As for now I've a different weapon
Stage and screen is about to beckon.

And here I sit in first class
Bollocks Sir, kiss my arse...

Jock Stein, the Celtic manager who was the first British manager to win the European cup agrees with the view that possibility and probability thinkers are able to determine your success. He said that the art of successfully creating a great player was to keep him away from the 8 team mates who hated the manager and would poison his thinking and steer him towards the other 2, who haven't made their minds up yet!

Now think about yourself.

If you were to list the names of the people who you spend most of your time with would you describe them as probability thinkers? If you need help in identifying them, listen out for these typical comments, which this sort of person specialises in:

"it will be a disaster; it always is!"

or, to quote Homer Simpson:

"you tried your best and failed miserably. The lesson is 'never try.'"

Are they the sort of people who boast about having 20 years experience but could, realistically, be said to have one years' experience which they have repeated 20 times? Are they people who respond to every idea with the words: "yes, but..."? Are they the people that the comedienne, Victoria Wood, had in mind when she said:

"man invented language only to satisfy his need to complain."

If so, then you're sat with probability thinkers.

Or do you sit with possibility thinkers?

They would typically comment:

"yeah, sounds good!"

These are people who look on the bright side and try to see the potential in things. They respond to every idea with the words: "yes and...". Frank Dick, the athletics coach, called them 'mountain people', because they love to rise to a challenge. Sir Isaac Newton, the man who defined the laws of gravity, referred to them in a letter to his friend, when he said:

"If I have seen further than others, it is because I was standing on the shoulders of giants."

Think about yourself. Are you a probability or a possibility thinker?

The US sociologist, Dr Wayne Dwyer, believes that we all belong to a number of different tribes at home, at work and socially. Each tribe operates within certain guidelines and traditions. Some of these are necessary, as they make sure that the tribe survives but many of its laws can hold the most talented people back as the speed of a tribe is slow and it moves at the speed of the slowest person and doesn't like one of its members learning something which is outside of its own laws.

Sir Matthew Pinsent, the four-times Olympic gold medal winner, explains this occurrence. When he was training, he and his 3 team mates would be wired up to static rowing machines and it would measure to check that they were all rowing at the same speed and with the same power. When they were all rowing in perfect harmony, the total result was that they were 110% more powerful. If one of the team dropped their rate by a fraction, subconsciously, the other three would drop as well, without even noticing.

"With a tired or weak team member, a boat will only go as fast as he allows it to go."

The message here is, who you surround yourself with is just as important as your own mental approach.

The next time you are sitting in the canteen and find one of your mates telling you that a task is impossible or that you are wasting your time chasing after something that you have identified as your purpose and goal, remember these words, which are the best example of someone who refused to listen to probability thinkers. Unfortunately, these probability thinkers included his national government and a whole nation, who told him that things couldn't and wouldn't change, no matter what he said or did. He was regarded as a dangerous fool and was imprisoned for remaining a possibility thinker.

"Our deepest fear is not that we are inadequate. Our deepest fear is that we are powerful beyond measure.

It is our light, not our darkness, that most frightens us. We ask ourselves, who am I to be ~ brilliant, gorgeous, talented and fabulous?

Actually, who are you not to be?

Your playing small doesn't serve the world. There is nothing enlightened about shrinking so small that other people won't feel insecure around you.

It's not just in us, it's in everyone.

As we let our own light shine, we unconsciously give other people permission to do the same. As we are liberated from our own fear, our presence automatically liberates others."

Nelson Mandela.

Action:

Identify which 'tribes' you belong to. Make a list of the people you spend most of your time with:

Now look at the people that are in these tribes and identify who are probability thinkers and who are possibility thinkers. Which group do you spend your time with?

Identify a group of people who you admire; people whom you believe can help you achieve your goals and who you can help achieve theirs. Commit to meet up and communicate on a regular basis to swap ideas and offer encouragement.

at home

at work

socially

Liquid thinkers

Gerry Fannon is an engineer from North West Liquids No.1 factory.

How did I get started?
I was working as a service engineer and was doing a lot of travelling around the country. I was regularly working 90 hour weeks and, one Friday, I was driving back home from London and took a short cut through some back country lanes, when I passed a boatyard.

I don't know why I did, but I suddenly decided to stop the car. Like I say, I still don't know why I did it but I parked up, got out and had a look around the different canal boats that were moored in the yard. Then, on impulse, I decided to hire one of the boats for a week there and then!

My first trip was a week's holiday on the canal boat with my wife and another couple of friends. We decided that we were going to sail to Market Drayton, in the Midlands but we had a pretty inauspicious start.

We were given an hour's training on how to open the lock of the canal but the training was given on a lock where the water level only rose and dipped by about 4 inches. Easy! After we had set sail, though, the first lock we came to was the major thoroughfare of 2 of the major canal routes in Britain, Trent and Mersey with the Shropshire union It was like learning to drive on a quiet, private country road and then having your test on a motorway. It will probably not surprise you to learn that we never did make it to Market Drayton but, by the end of that week, my ability to steer and open the locks, had improved massively. We were hooked. So much so, we booked

another week's holiday for the year after and were determined to make it to Market Drayton.

When we returned, we enjoyed another great week and although my confidence at controlling the boat had improved, we still didn't make it to our destination. We did, however, enjoy the whole experience so much, of being out in the countryside, enjoying the fresh air, watching the wildlife and finding hidden gems that you would never see from the roads, that we decided to save up and buy a canal boat, determined to fulfil our ambition of finally making it to the mythical land of Market Drayton. By the third year, we had our own boat and planned our trip in great detail, working out the route and everything else we needed to consider. It took us 2 1/2 weeks and the holiday was amazing and justified our decision to buy the boat. The biggest disappointment was that when we got to Market Drayton, it wasn't worth the effort! Think Ellesmere Port without the night-life or excitement.

Ultimate ambition.

We kept the boat for 7 years and had some brilliant holidays and memories on it. I also started to learn loads about the skills of canal boating. It was during these holidays that I started to think about what changes I'd make if I had the chance to build my own dream boat. Some of it was practical changes, such as making the engine easier to access, having central heating and improving the wiring and electrics. Some of it, though, was really radical. Most boats follow, roughly, the same design – they have a saloon, a kitchen, a bathroom and bedroom. They all look the same and I knew that I wanted something different, something unique, something that I could call mine.

I started going to the Ellesmere Port Boat Museum and began looking at the different styles of boats, that dated back some 200 years. I then started taking photos of different sorts of boats and nicking ideas that I'd seen on one boat and thinking about how I could adapt it to another. I drew diagrams and models, dozens and dozens of them, just putting down ideas and thinking about what it would look like, how practical it would be and what it would look like.

Liquid thinkers

I had already started taking photos of the boats and then did research at the library and on the internet about the practicalities of my ideas. Let me give you an example. Most modern boats are made of steel but I really liked the idea about how they used to make boats 100/150 years ago, which was to use planks of wood to construct the bow of the boat. I liked the idea that it would look old but would also be distinguished and unique. Also, most boats have fairly basic facilities like a shower and a toilet. In my dream boat, I wanted a large bath and a power-shower. If you are stood on the deck all the day in freezing weather, I can't think of anything better than to thaw out with a long soak in the bath. So, I drew that into my design.

Making it happen.

Once I'd decided what I wanted my dream boat to look like, I found some

guys who used to work at the Camel Laird shipyard and showed them my plans and designs. They certainly thought that it was unique and had never built anything like it before. They agreed to have a go at it. However, before they would give their full commitment, they insisted on building a model of it in plywood to see that it was possible. Once they had reassured themselves, and me, that it was possible, they gave me their agreement.

I would then go along to the shipyard every week, whenever I got the chance and would make amendments to the design as I saw it starting to take shape. For example, I'd wanted the boat to have portholes fitted into the sides but when they were in, I realised that it didn't let a lot of light in and so I added 'Houdini' hatches in the roof. Gradually, it started to take shape and started to look like my design.

It didn't go without its complications though. I had a really clear idea about where I wanted the engine to sit. I wanted it to go in the same place as on a trawler. This required using lots of angles and guesswork to position it in the right place and I got heavily involved at this stage and helped the lads work backwards from where I wanted the engine. After a lot of work, we finally managed to fit it and I was well happy with the result, as it gave me a lot more room. As it started to take shape, I continued to make amendments and change the design to fit in with the dream version and the costs started to creep up. My initial estimate of £25,000 ended up being dwarfed by the final amount of £37,000. My wife and I were committed to it, though, and we knew that it would be worth it. We found the extra funds.

The whole building project took over 2 years to finally complete and on the day I collected it, I arranged for it to be picked up by a low loader and taken to the wharf, where it was going to be lowered into the water by crane. By the time I'd made all the arrangements and finalised things, I arrived at the wharf and it was already in the water. It looked beautiful. The time was about 5pm and it was a 2/3 hour trip to the marina where it was going to be moored and so I decided that I was going to treat myself to a Chinese and a pint and I eventually ended up falling asleep on the deck. When I woke up, it was a lovely bright morning and I set off to the marina. Once I was nearly there, I gave my wife a call to tell her to get there so she could see the boat arrive. When she answered, she didn't seem too pleased to hear from me. It was 6 o'clock in the morning. I'd been so excited, I hadn't checked the time but had got up at 4 o'clock to set off!

The moment.

I can remember, exactly, the moment when I knew that all of the planning, preparation, saving and hard work had been worth it. It is crystallised in my mind.

We had gone to walk the dogs along the towpath and I looked back and saw my boat sitting amongst a number of others, all moored up. I remember thinking that if I were a passer-by, I would have picked out my boat as being the one I would have wanted. "That's our boat", I said to my wife. It looked class.

Future.

I'd like to live on the boat eventually and enjoy long cruises on it, to places like Oxford and Skipton. It's also an ambition to take it to the Albert Docks, when the canals there are re-opened. It would also be amazing to travel in it, along the canals and lakes of Ireland. The thing is, though, I will always be working to improve it. Once I get close to completing it, I will then start planning some other improvement.

Advice.

What advice would I give?

You should know what you want to achieve and should write it down and go back to it again and again to check that it is what you really want.

You should read up and do as much research as possible about what it is you want to achieve. You will be constantly amazed at the range of ideas which are out there. For example, in the 12 years since I started canal boating, technology has moved on in leaps and bounds and this research has allowed me to project my thinking forward and build it into my dream boat.

I'd also encourage anyone to fit your dream into the context of your whole life. this will allow you to decide how important it is to you and help you understand exactly why you want it. If you wanted to have your own canal boat for holidays only, you may not spend as much money or invest as much time into it as I did.

Finally, I urge you to enjoy learning an amazing amount along the way. I never dreamed that I'd acquire the skills which I have along the way, but it has been great fun.

Stop whaling

"My dear friend, clear your mind of can't."

Dr. Samuel Johnson,
the inventor of the
first ever dictionary

I recently read an article, which explained that William Shakespeare had used 17,676 different words in his plays. It also detailed that Shakespeare was responsible for inventing over 1,700 new words, such as 'critic', 'laughable', 'swagger', 'envy', 'elbow room' and 'moonbeam' into the English language. As you read this book, and think that it contains the 'naked truth', you would be using another phrase which he also created! On the other hand, if you are reading this and think that 'it's all Greek to me', well that's another of his creations, too.

To show that anyone can invent a word or a phrase, Sir Alex Ferguson has also managed to invent a new phrase by describing the pressure which players and managers feel at the end of season as 'squeaky bum time' and Iain Dowie, the Crystal Palace manager, has also found his way into the dictionary, by describing the ability to respond to set backs as, possessing 'bouncebackability!'

This idea of being able to invent words and phrases got me thinking. If something can be created and put into a dictionary, then surely words can be removed. Right?

If you want to achieve your purpose and goals in life, one lesson which all successful people share is the ability to take the word 'failure' out of their vocabulary and then behave like it doesn't exist. Ellen MacArthur, the youngest person and the fastest woman to sail around the world single-handedly, said:

"successful people usually snap success from seeming failure. If they know there is such a word as defeat or failure, they will not admit it. They may be whipped but they are not aware of it. That's why they succeed."

If failure doesn't exist for you, you can't fear it, can you? James Dyson first had the idea of inventing the bagless vacuum cleaner back in 1972, yet, you couldn't buy one in the UK until 1992. What was he doing for the 20 years in between? Let him explain:

"Failure seldom stops you. What stops you is the fear of failure. I have never encountered it, as I have only ever had temporary setbacks. Never walk away from these setbacks. On the contrary, study them carefully – and imaginatively – for their hidden assets. If you want to double your success rate, double your failure rate."

After he had finished playing, Jimmy Greaves was asked to explain how he had achieved the record of scoring 49 goals in a season for Tottenham Hotspur. He explained:

"I also got another, less well-known, record that same season. I got the record for the highest number of goals missed. I got this as I understood the lesson that I couldn't score every time I had a shot but I definitely wouldn't score, if I never even tried."

Greg Norman had the same attitude. In 1996, after losing the US Open to Nick Faldo, after he had been leading the field for the whole tournament, Norman was expected to sneak away quietly but instead he chose to face the whole world's media to explain that:

"losses aren't a waste of time. They are an apprenticeship. Real failure is a man who has blundered and not cashed in on the experience; failure is an attitude not an outcome."

Here's a question for you:

'Do you ever talk to yourself?'

As you read this book, listen to the voice in your head that you can hear now. This is what psychologists call your 'self talk' and so, the answer to the question is 'yes'.

Here is another question for you:

'Do you speak to your friends and family in the same way that you allow the voice in your head to speak to you?'

If you answered 'yes' to this second question, answer this third one:

'Do you have many family or friends left, that still speak to you?'

I mentioned in an earlier chapter that there are about two million pieces of information that are bombarding you every second. Here's another statistic for you. On average, you talk to yourself around ten thousand times a day. How many of the things which you say to yourself are positive messages and how many are negative? How many times do you find yourself saying 'I can't do that' or 'I'm an idiot'?

This voice in your head, your 'self talk', is the key to making you a success and to helping you achieve your goals.

Studies have been carried out with children from families whose the parents are working in professional industries and children from families, whose parents are on social benefits. Up until the age of four, the children from professional families, have received 700,000 positive comments, such as 'well done' and 'excellent' and have only received 80,000 negative comments, such as 'stop it' or 'don't do that'.

In contrast, children from families on benefits have, by the same age, received 60,000 positive comments compared to 120,000 negative ones.

In summary, the 'professional kids' will hear seven times as many positive comments as opposed to negative ones, whereas 'benefits kids' will hear twice as many negative statements than positive ones.

This statistic is cited as a huge factor in determining how successful a child will be in later years.

The great thing is that it's never too late to stop and reverse this. Ask yourself, again, what is the proportion of positive rather than negative comments which you tell yourself every day?

Try this technique. Start to monitor what you say to yourself and substitute phrases like, 'I can't' for 'I won't' (can you see the distinction between this? It is back to the whole matter of choice, which is where we started this book.) Stop telling yourself that 'I'll try' and instead tell yourself that 'I'll choose to/I'll choose not to'.

Think of Yoda, the wise old Jedi master, who told Luke Skywalker, when he expressed doubts about his ability to beat Darth Vader and conquer the Dark Side:

"Either do or do not. There is no try."

This reminds me of a story related to me by Jimmy Meadows, about a TPM course he once attended in the factories:

"A positive something is better than a negative nothing. There were several operators and engineers present for this course and the instructor radiated positive thinking as he spoke, and thought, only in terms of the impossibility of failure and the certainty of success.

We were given a test in what we had learned so far and, as we did it, one or two of us began to discuss the problems we had encountered. The instructor wasn't having any of that and he said: "let me make one thing perfectly clear, gentlemen. In the world of TPM there are no such things as problems only opportunities!"

There was a pause and then one of the guys in the far corner said, very gently, *"In that case, I wonder if you would give me a hand with an insurmountable opportunity?"*

Start to change your own language.

Action:

Make yourself accountable for your internal dialogue. 80% of our emotions come from how we talk to ourselves.

Start to monitor what you say in your head and then make yourself a promise that you won't say anything in your head that you wouldn't allow a stranger to say to you.

Count how many times you say out loud that you 'can't' do something or how useless you are and then aim to reduce it.

Train yourself to ask better questions then asking yourself why you can't do something or when you are beating yourself up for not achieving something. Think about a situation where something has gone wrong for you and ask yourself the following questions:

i. How important will this be in a couple of months time?

ii. Is my response appropriate and effective?

iii. How can I influence or improve the situation?

iv. What can I learn from it?

v. What will I do differently next time?

vi. What can I find that is positive in this situation?

Practise asking these questions next time you are faced with a similar situation and notice how it starts to effect the results you get..

Go fishing

You are never going to get everything right first time, in fact Winston Churchill summed it up when he said: *"striving for excellence motivates you; striving for perfection demoralises you"*

Did you know that, according to the business guru, Tom Peters, the Sony Corporation takes about 5 days to go from having an idea to having something, which they can test in the marketplace. Compare this to most companies who, on average, take 11 months to achieve the same thing.

Why is there such a difference? It would appear that Sony are not chasing perfection. They are looking for feedback, which it can take and build into its next efforts.

Don't aim for perfection. Give yourself permission to be imperfect.

Just as important is the question of who you choose to listen to. Look back to the earlier chapter about who you associate with: possibility or probability thinkers and think about the people with whom you surround yourself with. Sir Alex Ferguson claims that he takes advice from everybody but rarely uses it, unless it comes from an achiever.

"By achiever, I don't necessarily mean someone who has scored a mountain of goals or won every trophy available. I don't care

which path they have gone down, so long as they've done the walking. That way, you know that they know the consequences – the price. People who know those things, rarely talk rubbish."

It is critically important to go fishing for feedback from people who will give constructive criticism rather than false praise or damning dismissal from *"those poor spirits, who neither enjoy much or suffer much because they live in that great twilight that knows not victory or defeat."* (Theodore Roosevelt).

Richard Branson has identified the people that matter to him, his customers, as an important source of feedback.

"Whenever I'm on a flight or train or in a record store, I ask people for their ideas on how to improve the service. I write them down and when I get home, look through what I've written. If there's a good idea, I implement it."

Take regular feedback and take it from those who matter.

Action:

Keep track of your progress and how many attempts that you make at achieving your goal.

Don't claim:

"I've must've tried 100 times to improve or change things"

and count whether it is really once or twice before you gave up.

Share your goals with people and ask for feedback in as many forms as possible (written, verbal, etc.) from as many different people as possible as regular as possible.

Finally, practise being gracious in your response to feedback.

Make it easy for people to offer it.

Liquid thinkers

Paul Lee is the Planning Leader for North West Liquids.

What is your ambition?
It's a good question isn't
it and it's only since I sat
down to contribute to this
book, I have had chance
to sit and think about my
answer to this question.

How did I go from being a raw 19
year old football player to being a well
respected rugby club captain standing
in front of a room packed with rugby
colleagues and successfully delivering a
speech to over 200 of them? It was a hell
of a journey! Let me tell you a bit about
it and what I learned along the way.

I was a pretty good footballer and had
even had trials for Everton. I was playing
twice a weekend and once during the
week. It was during the summer close
season that I decided to go along to my
local rugby club, Old Instonians, just to
keep fit, in anticipation of the football
season starting again.

A lot of the training involved loads of
running and at this stage I had, quite
literally, never picked up a rugby ball
before. After I had been going along to
the fitness sessions for a few weeks,
one of the blokes running the training
asked me whether I fancied joining in
the practise games. I'm a big lad, anyway,
and they thought that I could stand in as
a second row. After a bit of persuading,
I agreed to give it a go. I actually enjoyed
it more than I thought I would. I carried
on going along to the training and
joining in the games until, eventually,
they asked me if I'd like to play for the
3rd XV.

I still regarded myself as a footballer,
first and foremost, but I agreed to play
for them and help them out where
I could. So, for a few years, I fitted
in playing rugby around my football
commitments. It was only when I got
to 21, that I finally understood and knew
exactly what I wanted to do and achieve
in rugby.

I got invited along to one of the club
dinners and I can vividly recall seeing
the club captain stand up, at the top
table, and deliver a fantastic speech to a
packed audience. What really sticks out
in my mind, was the respect which he
seemed to command from everyone in
that room. I looked around me and saw
the faces of people sitting rapt at what
he had to say. I noticed that the banter,
which is always pretty near-the-knuckle
at these do's, was tinged with a real
respect towards this guy.

I knew, there and then, that if I was
going to carry on playing rugby, I didn't
want to be just a rugby player. I wanted
to go one step further and become a
rugby club captain.

Liquid thinkers

In rugby, the role of the captain is really different from football. You are responsible for selecting the team, for giving the team talks, deciding the tactics and hosting the other teams when they visit you and acting as the ambassador for your club, when you visit others. It is more similar, in lots of ways, to the role of a manager of a football team. You are responsible for setting the tone of the behaviour and attitudes within your club. The position is regarded as a real honour and privilege. To be given it, you must be elected by the players and the committee members. They must believe you have the sort of qualities to carry out these tasks, as well as being good enough to make sure you are selected for the 1st team.

If you'd asked me then, at this stage – remember, I was still only coming along for a laugh and was still trying to learn how to play the game – how I was going to become a member of the 1st team, let alone captain them, I wouldn't have had a clue. It is only now, with the benefit of hindsight and experience that I can recognise what motivated me. It was the picture of imagining myself as captain, exuding respect and self-confidence, which motivated me towards what must have looked like a pipe dream.

How did I manage it then? I carried on the commitment of coming along to the training sessions and I kept on improving my skills in the second row and listening to the help and advice

which the other players gave me, until I made it into the 1st XV. Over the next few years, I managed to establish myself as an important part of this team and kept on improving my game by regular practice and hard work.

The club captaincy is held for two years and before the current captain had to stand down, I spoke with my mates and they agreed to support me when I stood for election. I put myself up and was awarded the position. This wasn't enough, though. I wanted to feel like I could achieve the levels of respect and credibility that I had enviously felt, years earlier, and I knew that it would take me a while longer to get this.

There were times when the role was tough and I considered packing it in. One example stands out. In my first year, there was a lot of backbiting and moaning about selection issues and so I had to close the dressing room doors and have some blunt conversations with the team. I put an end to the complaining and we started to work together as a team. In later years, friends of mine have told me that my honesty and my willingness to face up to these issues really started to help me become established and achieve the respect which I craved.

You may read this and think that my ambition is a bit vague, because it was centred more around a feeling than something you could measure, but I can remember the exact moment when I knew that I had got there and knew that I had managed to get the status I had wanted so badly from that first club dinner.

Over the next few years, I had moved to different clubs a couple of times and was elected as club captain on both occasions. I was playing for Old Parkonians against my other old team, Prenton. In rugby, there can be a lot of funny business (punching, gouging, biting, that sort of thing) which goes on in the rucks and the mauls. On this day, during that game, none of this went on. There was no underhand methods and it was played in a really hard but fair way. We won and the opposing captain came up to me afterwards and admitted that we had given them a real beating. There was a real respect, which I felt that my old team had given me, in accepting that it would be tough but in not resorting to cheating. The feeling of knowing that I had gained that level of respect was amazing and gave me a real thrill.

What did I learn which I could pass on to anyone else about going for your ambitions?

There's a couple of pieces of advice. The main one is that you will have doubts about whether you can do it but the reality of a situation will very rarely be as bad as your doubts.

Secondly, I'd say, don't wait for chances to come along. Go for it. 9 times out of 10 you will get an answer of some sort or another, which will help you move forward towards your goal.

Finally, remember to enjoy what you're doing along the way.

Think in watercolour

"*We are not retreating,
we are merely attacking
in another direction.*"

Major General
Oliver Smith

There are no rules for creativity. Here are five guidelines that, when we follow them, will mean that we tend to come up with fresher, more innovative ideas.

Go for quantity.

"I find that the best way to have a good idea, is to have lots of them", remarked the two times Nobel Prize winner Linus Pauling.

When it comes to creativity, more is better, partly because we never know when we are going to hit on something great and partly, because by going for volume, we force ourselves to think more widely than just about our immediate problem.

Don't judge or evaluate the ideas as you go along.

This is the hardest rule to stick to. No sooner do we have some seemingly absurd thought than we dismiss it as, well, absurd. All ideas are good ideas, because at the time we have them, we don't know where they might lead us to.

Write down or capture in some way all the ideas you have.

If you don't put them down, you may end up concentrating on just trying to remember what you've already thought of, rather than putting the ideas, however brilliant, to one side and thinking afresh.

Learn to love half answers.

The moment of genius may come from letting an earlier thought that you liked (but couldn't quite put your finger on why you liked it) take shape and form in your mind. Ambiguity is great. Don't dismiss partial solutions as they can often lead you to the complete answer, even though, frustratingly, it may not be straight away.

Be naïve.

Even the most experienced panel of experts can miss the answer to a dilemma precisely because they apply their experience. They are able to identify all of the complex difficulties obstructing their normal procedure but by being naïve in your approach, you may be alert to the existence of another approach altogether.

One story that captures this point perfectly is the classic tale of the lorry that got stuck under a bridge. A crowd gathered and had a number of suggestions. Some suggested tearing the top off the lorry, others said dismantle the bridge. The argument raged back and forth until a small child at the back asked: ' Why don't you let the air out of the tyres?'

Have an objective.

This is the most important point and relates back to the purpose of this book. Aimless creativity is usually just that. Always keep in mind your sense of purpose as this greatly increases the odds of you coming up with something that is not only original but also worthwhile.

Many inventions which we take for granted today had the strangest of beginnings. For example:

The roll-on deodorant. The original deodorant was invented back in 1888 in Philidelphia but it wasn't until the 1950's that the roll-on appeared. The inspiration? The ballpoint pen. An inventive employee worked out that the same idea could be used to spread the deodorant evenly, as it could for ink.

The microwave oven. This invention came about as a by-product of World War II radar research. Whilst working on magnetrons (vacuum tubes that produce microwave radiation), engineer, Percy Lebarron Spencer, discovered that a chocolate bar in his pocket had melted. Working out that the microwaves were the cause, he experiented and discovered that, not only could microwaves cook food, they could do so much faster than a normal oven.

The alcopop. This came about because an Australian farmer was throwing away a large proportion of his lemon crop, simply because the lemons weren't the right size. rather than letting these rot, his neighbour, a brewer, took them and used his knowledge of brewing and a family recipe for lemonade, and the 'Two Dogs' lemon brew was created.

If you always do what you've always done, you will always get what you've always got. Be creative in your journey towards your goals.

Action:

Answer these two questions:

Were you a kid once?

Do you dream?

The answer to these 2 questions is 'yes' and they prove that you are both creative and innovative.

Think of the games and activities you used to play as a kid during the long summer holidays, for example, you may have dreamt of playing for your favourite team at Wembley in a cup final. Make a list.

What you dream about now? In the earlier chapter – 'are you a drifter?' – you answered what you would do if you won the lottery. Look back at this list.

You may dream that you would travel the world if you suddenly became rich. Now, start to be creative and think about where and how you could travel without being a millionaire!

Finally, go back to your goal, which you wrote in the 'liquid goal-d' chapter. Write down as many ways as you can think of, about how you can achieve it.

Apply the creative principles detailed above.

The answer will be out there.

Swim against the tide

"*Nothing in the world can take the place of persistence. Talent will not – nothing is more common than an unsuccessful man with talent. Genius will not – unrewarded genius is almost a proverb. Education will not – the world is full of educated derelicts. Persistence and determination alone, are all powerful.*"

Ray Kroc, the man who founded McDonalds

Research into sales has shown that 73% of customers say 'no' five times before they say 'yes'. Further research shows that only 8% of salespeople ever go past being told 'no' five times or more. Do the maths. This means that 8% of people are getting 73% of business, so, no wonder they go on to become the most successful people in an organisation and it is the same with you and your dreams. How many of us just give up the first time we get a 'no'?

Perseverance is not about doing the same thing over and over. It also requires the courage to look at yourself and change your habits.

In the days, when the only car which Ford sold were open-topped model Ts, all of the dealers throughout America were told to close during the winter. Henry Ford, the head of the company, reasoned that you wouldn't be able to sell open-topped cars at this miserable time of year. During the winter break, Henry Ford decided to do a tour of his most successful dealers to see how he could offer any help or advice for when they re-opened in the summer. He arrived at his most successful dealership – a place that sold twice as many cars as their nearest rival – during a heavy snow storm. He was surprised to find it open. He summoned the manager and asked him what he thought he was doing, selling cars in the middle of the winter. The manager replied: "Sorry, Mr Ford, nobody ever told us we had to close."

Now you have identified your purpose and your goals, as you start to move towards them, you may not see the results instantly and start to feel that it is not worth pursuing.

Frank Dick, the coach of Boris Becker, Linford Christie and Daley Thompson, was the head coach of the British track and field team throughout the 1980's. It took a long time before they tasted any success before the team went on to win the European Cup in 1989, which was the first time this had been achieved.

When journalists asked Dick how he had done it, he explained that it was down to the preparation and work which had been done years before, which had led to this great achievement. He explained it by using the story of the Chinese bamboo:

"The Chinese bamboo plant, when it is planted, doesn't do anything in the first year. It doesn't even sprout a single green shoot; nothing. It is the same in the second year. And the third year and the fourth, yet, in the fifth year, in a space of 6 weeks, the bamboo will grow to be over 90 feet high. The question is, did it grow 90 feet in 6 weeks or in 5 years? It proves that persistence does pay off."

Harrison Ford was in Hollywood for 14 years and was working as a carpenter, before he was offered a some acting work. He said:

"It took me 14 years to become an overnight success. "

The actress and model, Sophia Loren, spent many similar years, facing rejection and being advised to quit and get a normal job. She said:

"Getting ahead requires avid faith in yourself. You must be able to sustain yourself against staggering blows and unfair reversals. When I think back to my first years in Rome, those endless rejections, without a glimmer of encouragement from anyone, all those failed screen tests and yet I never let my desire slide away from me, my belief in myself and what I felt I could achieve."

A great example of persistence is the cyclist Miguel Indurain. The first time he rode the Tour de France, he finished 90th. The next year he finished 40th, then 19th, then 10th. By the 5th year, he finally won it and he continued to do so for the following five years. He says:

"Within us all is a message which we tend to overlook: most of us have highs and lows but its the perseverance, the determination, at the day's end that makes us what we are. It is not about being smarter or having more opportunities, as others will tell you. Those who won't take the risk of failing and go for it, who won't see things out, they're the ones who come home early, never answering the challenge and never going anywhere."

When you have committed to your goals, rejection will come your way. Expect it. Welcome it. Cherish it. Then ignore it and carry on.

Action:

Commit to being
unstoppable.
Tell yourself, every day,
that you are unstoppable.

What made Stuart Pearce take a crucial
penalty for England in Euro '96 when
he had already experienced the pain
after missing one 6 years earlier against
Germany, which saw his team lose the
semi-final?

Pearce says that he had banished his fear
of failure and so was prepared to take a
risk in order to dare to be successful.

This fear makes us stop taking risks and
start playing conservatively and small.
As Nelson Mandela asks:

"Why should you not be brilliant,
gorgeous, talented and fabulous?"

Make a promise to yourself to become
unstoppable and to keep it.

*Think of a example of of
where you have exceeded
your own expectations.*

Liquid thinkers

Steve Byrne is an engineer for North West Liquids.

When I was a young apprentice, I worked alongside an older guy who used to speak about his goal of building his own home but he never did get around to doing it. This was when the idea took hold and stayed in the back of my mind, but it was never something that I'd never discussed seriously with anyone, not even with Karen, my wife.

When I look back now, this thought was obviously still there in my mind when we were looking around for a house in 1996. This was one of my life long ambitions and I had a chance of making it happen.

When we saw one place, it looked like the Adams family house, it was so desperately run down, but there was something about it which made me go back and look beyond the surface and consider its potential. It had a huge plot of land attached which provided us with some scope to build on it. After a bit of thought, we went ahead and purchased the house and moved in that year. Even at this point Karen was not aware of what I had in mind and what I was planning.

By 2001, Alicia, my second daughter had been born and the house was starting to feel too small for a family of 4. My eldest, Charlotte, had started at a good school and was really enjoying it and we wanted both of them to be educated there. Unfortunately, the local council had implemented a restriction which meant that you had to live in the local area to qualify for a place there. The house prices in that area were pretty steep and so we had a clear choice: either find the money to move to the area or uproot my eldest so both of them could go to the same school. We didn't want to take this second option, as the education of my girls' is of the utmost importance to me and so it seemed as good a time as any to bring up the idea that had been germinating in my mind for years and I suggested the idea of building a house on the land, selling both, which would allow us to generate the cash to move to the appropriate area. We had to do this by 2005, if we were to achieve our aims. It didn't turn out that simple.

I spoke with Karen and it seemed like a powerful reason to want to do it. There were only two real problems:

I had no experience of building and didn't have a clue about where to start and;

we didn't have any spare money.

We decided to go ahead with our plans anyway...

Liquid thinkers

BOMBSHELL No.1

The only asset of any value which I had was my beloved motorbike and I put it up for sale to signal my serious intent to the family and we used the money to pay for an architect to draw up plans. We all got involved in helping design the layout of the house. It looked fabulous and we excitedly submitted it to the council for the necessary planning permission.

We received a reject letter back from them, politely explaining that we had a Tree Preservation Order on an old oak tree, which proudly stood at the bottom of the garden. We were undeterred and went back to the drawing board with our architect and re-submitted our revised plans. The response was a little more encouraging. They said that if we could receive confirmation from a tree surgeon that the oak tree wouldn't be damaged by the building work, we could go ahead. I was watching the money from the sale of my bike being quickly eroded but the tree surgeon confirmed that our plans

were sound. We got back to the council, who insisted that we pay for their tree surgeon to double-check.12 months had passed, by the time we had found our way through this bureaucratic maze.

BOMBSHELL No.2

The next stage of our plan was pretty simple. We needed to borrow £100,000 from a finance company. This would allow us to build the shell of the house. After this, I would take responsibility for building the rest of the place, including fitting out the whole of the interior. We went round quite a few companies and were met with a lot of refusals. One or two of them suggested that we needed to sell the house we were living in to raise the money. This wasn't an option. Not only did I not want to disrupt the family, we didn't actually have anywhere to move to in the interim. We needed to build the house before we could sell our current home. It was a 'catch 22' situation.

BOMBSHELL No.3

It was September 2003 before the Nationwide building society agreed, in principle, to lend us the required amount, as long as we were able to show them the costings, the plans, insurance and a welter of other documents which proved that we knew what we were doing. It felt like we were on our way!

I had already started discussions with the builders we planned to use and they explained that unless they started the building work in the October, it was likely to be another 6/7 months before he would be able to fit us in again. In addition, they explained that as winter was approaching, we needed to get the foundations down before the poor weather set in. I didn't have the final approval from the Nationwide but they had given me their agreement, in principle. I had to balance up the options. We couldn't afford to delay the building work if we were to meet our 2005 deadline against the fact that I didn't have the final approval for the funding. I can still remember the date when I crossed the Rubicon. It was October 18th 2003 and I came home from work to find a bloody big JCB digger churning up my garden and I knew that there was no going back. Besides, the approval from the building society would be arriving any day now.

However, a couple of weeks later, I got one of those phone calls, which you dread, from the Nationwide explaining that they had lost my application. I had to resubmit all of the information again and face another month-long wait for approval. In the meantime, I had to find £10,000 to pay the builders for the first month's work. I chased around and arranged a short-term loan from my bank.

It was the week before Christmas when I finally heard back off the Nationwide. The guy on the phone cheerfully informed me that they wouldn't be lending me the money and, he, helpfully added that he didn't think that there was a company in existence that would lend us the amount we needed. As he was speaking, the image of that JCB digging my garden up danced before my eyes. I was poleaxed.

I recovered myself and managed, somehow, to put a brave face on for the sake of the girls, so that they could enjoy Christmas. I kept thinking about where I could find some positives from the mess I was in. The only comfort was that the builders had taken 2 weeks off for Christmas and so I didn't have to pay them. I was in too deep to go back but I would lie awake at night, the feeling of panic rising up in me. Karen began to recognise the fear I was feeling. She suggested that we back out completely and call off the builders. It was tempting but I was determined to find a way around the problem and continue. The resulting stress caused conflict in our marriage.

BOMBSHELL No.4

It was a chance conversation with my sister-in-law in the bleak January of 2004 that offered a slim glimmer of hope. She works for the Halifax and she mentioned that she knew a friend of a friend that might be able to lend us the money. By this time, my debt, which I had borrowed to pay the men working on the house had risen to £57,000 and the interest payments from various bank loans were starting to spiral out of control.

The Halifax agreed to lend the money on the proviso that the Abbey, the company with whom I had a mortgage on my current property, would agree to split the land. The Abbey sent a surveyor round to value the land to see if that was worth more than the mortgage I held with them. If this surveyor said 'yes', I would get my loan. If he said 'no', I was in serious trouble with no obvious way out. It marked the start of the longest, most sleepless and stressful week of my life. When the letter dropped through my letter box in March 2004, I hesitated briefly before I dared to open it. I knew that I was holding more than a letter in my hand. I was holding £58,000 worth of spiralling debt, a half-built house, land and an existing house that were seriously devalued and a marriage that was coming under severe strain and all because of some idea that I'd been incubating for years. When I opened it, the relief flooded over me like a wave.

It said 'yes'. I had a quiet moment alone where I thought that we must have used up our share of bad luck by now.

Liquid thinkers

BOMBSHELL No.5

The building work could continue and we got the shell up in three months. We then got the first house on the market, in order to pay back the loans and it sold within a week. I started to think that our luck had started to turn. We agreed a completion date of August, which gave us a 3 month deadline to transform the shell to a state which we could live in. I had a target and I threw myself into it. I'd come home every evening, get changed and work until it turned dark, seven days a week, furiously driving myself on to complete it. Every spare minute I had was spent engrossed in working on our home. I learned how to carry out the plumbing installation and I assisted in the work on the electrics, plastering and flooring.

A significant moment, which had a deep and lasting effect on me and my attitude came one Saturday.

I was hammering away whilst my daughters were playing with their friends in the sand downstairs. I could half hear their conversations and I caught one of Charlotte's friends' comment: "I wish my daddy could build a house". My eldest daughter's reply stopped me dead. "You wouldn't, Beth" she said "I don't see my dad." I stopped what I was doing and lots of thoughts went through my mind. I remembered my dad, who had worked at Levers for 40 years – the last 15 of which were working nights – and remembered how much I had missed him and I thought 'what have I done?'

I realised that in my desire to reach my goal and build a dream house, the whole family had suffered, especially my wife, who had never complained but had continued to support me and keep the family moving without my help. That day, I resolved to myself that when I had finished this house, I would make up for my months of absence to Karen and the girls.

BOMBSHELL No.6

Whilst this was all going on, I was helping my parents move house. During this period, my dad suffered a heart attack. It seemed like one thing after another. Where would it end?

BOMBSHELL No.7

Immediately after we had sold our house, we paid £1000 to a company to arrange to have all of the services – gas, electricity, water, etc. – installed. The waiting list for this is about 3 months and so it fitted neatly within the timescales we were working towards. In the October, however, we received a phone call from the management of this company. They were deeply apologetic but the agent we had been dealing with had just been dismissed for fraud. He had taken our money but had made absolutely no arrangements to have the services fitted. We faced another 3 months' wait and we, therefore, suddenly had no home which we could live in, as we had to move from our current house within the week or face huge financial penalties for breaching the contract.

We ended up moving into my mother-in-law's house, where the girls had to sleep on the floor in sleeping bags whilst we cramped ourselves up in a small box room. During the three months we stayed here, the girls would ask when we could go home. I just felt so helpless. This was a nightmare.

WHAT HAPPENED NEXT?

In December 2004, just before my deadline of 2005, we eventually moved into the newly built house and had another couple of tough weeks, where we had to borrow water off the neighbours until we had our own supply fitted and we decided that after everything we had been through, we should live in the house for at least 12 months before facing the stress of another move.

At the same time, my youngest daughter was allowed to move to the school we wanted, which removed the pressure of having to move home immediately. My dad recovered fully from his heart attack and both him and my mum moved into their new home, where they are happy and settled. Most importantly, my relationship with my family is now stronger than ever. Before, I would sit and read a magazine and have a ready excuse for the kids if they wanted me to go and play with them. Now, I think back to that day when I heard the hurt in Charlotte's voice and enjoy getting up and playing with them. For Karen and I, we have been through so much stress and turmoil, we now know that there is nothing we can't deal with together. And what about me? I sometimes allow myself a long soak in the bath and time to reflect on the great sense of pride and belief which building the house around me has given me. It gives me a real, deep sense of satisfaction. I have learnt so much, including the knowledge that nothing can stress me out anymore as well as the deep-rooted belief that I could attempt anything, if I really want it enough.

ADVICE

Karen asked me, if I'd had a crystal ball, back in 2003, and could know what would happen over the next 2 years, would I have still gone ahead with it. My answer is a undoubted and resounding 'yes'. My purpose was to be the best dad and husband I could possibly be and my goal – to build a house for the family – was very clear. If you have this knowledge, there is nothing, not illnesses, lies, setbacks or overwhelming odds, that can't be overcome with belief and persistence.

Dive in!

There are two ways to climb a tree.
1. Climb it.
2. Sit on an acorn and wait for it to grow.

Now you have identified your purpose, written your goal, committed to it and fallen in love with it, do something, however small, which takes you a step in the direction of achieving it.

Time does not wait for any of us. Don't wait for circumstances to be perfect.

The station   by Robert J. Hastings

Tucked away in our subconscious is an
idyllic vision.
We see ourselves on a long trip that
spans the continent.
We are travelling by trains. Out of the
windows we drink
in the passing scenes of cars on nearby
highways, or children
waving at a passing crossing, of cattle
grazing on a distant hillside, of
smoke pouring from a power plant,
of row upon row of corn and
wheat, of flatlands and valleys,
of mountains and rolling hillsides
of city skylines and village halls.

But uppermost in our mind is the
final destination.
On a certain day at a certain hour,
we will pull into the station.
Bands will be playing and flags waving.
Once we get there so many
wonderful dreams will come true and
pieces of our lives will
fit together like a completed jigsaw puzzle.
How restlessly we pace
the aisles damning the minutes for
loitering waiting, waiting
waiting for the station.

"When we reach the station, that will
be it!" We cry!
"When I'm 18". "When I buy the new
450 SL Mercedes Benz!"
"When I put the last kid through college."
"When I have paid off
the mortgage!" "When I reach the age
of retirement I shall live happily ever
after!"

Sooner or later we must realise that there
is no station, no one place to arrive at once
and for all. The true joy of life is the trip.
The station is only a dream. It constantly
outdistances us.

"Relish the moment" is a good motto...
Forget the regrets over yesterday and
the fear of tomorrow.
Regret and fear are twin thieves who
rob us of today.

So, stop pacing the aisles and counting
the miles.
Climb more mountains, eat more ice
cream, go barefoot more often,
forge more,
watch more sunsets, laugh more, cry less.
Life must be lived as we go along. The
station will come soon enough.

Personal postscript

I have always wanted to write a book. I wasn't bothered what sort, biography, fiction, sci-fi, real-life stories, it didn't really matter. I just loved the idea of sitting down alone and translating my thoughts onto a piece of paper. I had never even given any thought as to who would bother to read my words. It was the concept of writing that appealed to me.

I can now recognise that this was the problem. There was no purpose to it. If I didn't know what I would write about, let alone who I would write for, where was the motivation to do anything about it?

Over the last few years, I have thought about writing a book quite a bit and have even become quite eloquent about my intentions to write. In fact, it is one of the first topics of conversation with my partner, Geraldine, when we go away on holiday. You know those first few days when you start to unwind and enjoy getting used to the fact that the days are your own, to fill however you want? Well, this is normally the moment when I come back to one of my favourite topics, writing a book. I have sat in café's, bars and restaurants from the balmy beaches of Copacabana to the frozen landscapes of Reykjavik and bored Geraldine with my intention that this was the holiday when I would start to put pen to paper. She has even learned the art of silencing this looped conversation by challenging me with the question 'what will you write about?' I tend to mumble a reply of 'er, I'm not sure' before looking to quickly change the topic.

I started work in Port Sunlight in May 2004, as the Human Resources Manager for North West Liquids. During my first few weeks, I had the chance to spend some time helping out and getting to meet some of the people that worked on the lines and in the warehouse. During break times, we would chat about our weekend, hobbies and families and I noticed that there was one common thread that ran through every conversation. Everyone I spoke with had a passion, something which they cared deeply about and enjoyed.

I met one lad who was a keen bodybuilder. It turned out that he competed at it. Now, I don't know the first thing about bodybuilding but when we started chatting, I started to appreciate the different characteristics that were required for it. It needed discipline in order to get up and go training 3 or 4 times a week; it required a high degree of analysis to be able to judge your diet accurately enough to come into competition looking your best. Finally, to put yourself up against others must require a healthy level of competitiveness. What I also noticed was that when we spoke, the lad came alive, bubbled with enthusiasm and passion. He cared about it. He wasn't the only one.

As I started to get to grips with my job, I remembered the conversations I had enjoyed in my first few months and thought that if only we could do something that could tap into those depths of passion, skills and characteristics, we would be able to improve the performance of North

West Liquids. After all, if you are doing something that you think can help or support your passion, you are more likely to care about it and do it well. It struck me that it was within my command to do something.

At the start of the year, I launched a Training Academy in the factories. My aim was to offer everyone the opportunity to develop themselves in some way and help them to be brilliant at their job. I also wanted to offer the chance to meet others who were brilliant at their chosen profession and so I started inviting a guest speakers to come in every month and talk about their careers and how they had successfully achieved their goals and ambitions.

It didn't matter how diverse each speaker was, there were a number of common characteristics and techniques which they all employed on their journey to success. Karen Darke, the lady who was paralysed at 21 before she cycled across the Himalayas identified the need to possess a clear goal as did Robin Reid, the world champion boxer who was drawn to the sport to achieve self respect. Sir John Jones, the headmaster who turned around Britain's worst school, recognised the need to change his and his pupils' beliefs regarding their own ability as much as Chris Moon had to, when facing up to his disability. Fergus Finlay, the man responsible for bringing the Special Olympics to Ireland echoed other guests in acknowledging the importance of persistence.

As I started to see the common threads, the idea for my book started to emerge as a realistic opportunity. It had all of the right ingredients. I wanted to write a book, I was passionate about the subject matter and enjoyed researching and reading books, plus it could be unique and special due to the rich resource I had exclusive access to – the people of North West Liquids.

As I began to capture the themes which bound all of these achievers together, I recognised that I should also adopt them. If I was going to write about it, I should be able to say, with all honesty, that I had also employed the same techniques. This book is a testimony to the principles that are contained in it.

I knew that I had previously lacked focus about writing and didn't have a target. This time, I wrote down, on a postcard, my goal. I then put the postcard in my diary and used it as a bookmark. I knew I would see it every day and that it would motivate me to take at least one step a day that moved me closer towards my goal.

I have written a book about personal success and the techniques to achieve it. I have used lots of examples from famous achievers in order to make and highlight the points but have interweaved stories of North West Liquids employees amongst it, to demonstrate that these techniques are open and available for us all to use. I have published it in December 2005 and have distributed to all North West Liquids employees in January 2006.

I wrote to people who I regard as heroes or achievers in their own chosen fields and asked them for their opinions on what techniques and characteristics were present when success happened. Mike Finnigan, the founder of 'Advance', a company that does a lot of work with Everton and Bolton Wanderers focusing on the importance of adopting a positive attitude, gave up time to sit and discuss his experiences with me. Sir John Jones sat and discussed the characteristics he had recognised in his years of teaching and helping to salvage desperate situations. My Dad, who is a word class boxing trainer and his fighters gave their views on the difference between success and failure.

More great advice and support came from an unlikely source, a visit to the doctors. I was sat in the waiting room, flicking through the magazines that were on display and read an article by a sports psychologist, called Martin Perry, who wrote an incisive and thought provoking article on the techniques which Jose Mourinho had adopted to bring success to Chelsea. I wrote his name in my notebook and I resolved to contact him. I wrote to the magazine and sent an e-mail to him, explaining what I was doing and asking him for his help, support and opinions. He agreed to come and meet with me and has offered a number of insights and views for the book.

Winston Churchill once said that "it is a good thing for an uneducated man to read books of quotations", and I have always tried to take that advice on board and so when I read a book, I do so with a notebook nearby. I am a collector of quotes and stories which I can use either in work or in coaching and once I had identified 14 of the most important techniques for achieving success I included in this book the stories, anecdotes and facts from my reading. It's funny but once I knew what I was looking for, I started to see loads of other examples in every walk of life (a great example of my RAS working) such as in films, magazines, interviews and adverts.

In the course of my job, I have met a number of fascinating people who have told me their stories. I approached some of them and explained my purpose and invited them to contribute. It staggered me that everyone I asked were so eager to help and offer up their stories with honesty and candour. They made me feel inspired on the evenings when I came home and couldn't face sitting down to write.

I knew that I needed to show my work to others and get feedback. I asked Geraldine to give me her honest assessment and she was as good as her word. Unfortunately, I wasn't quite prepared for such honesty and felt incredibly protective as she made a number of constructive criticisms. Eventually, we agreed on a compromise; she would continue to read the drafts and give feedback but I would listen and consider them for a few hours before responding. 90% of the time I accepted them and made the changes but it taught me an important lesson about myself and about feedback. I had to adjust my thinking to be able to accept it.

When you are clear about what you want to achieve, there will be an incredible amount of opportunities that present themselves. For example, I attended a course about organisational design. What could possibly be of benefit to my book on such a course? However, during it, two incredibly talented cartoonists came and produced fantastic illustrations throughout the days. I was amazed and fascinated by their brilliance and approached Nicky and Andrew. They agreed to animate and design my book.

Finally, I wanted to get a foreword for this book from someone like Muhammad Ali, an icon that embodied a lot of the techniques in it. How was I, writing a book in my spare time, ever going to approach someone like Ali to help me out? I started from my goal and worked backwards, thinking about how I could reach it. My Dad knew a man that knew a man that knew Angelo Dundee, Ali's trainer and coach throughout his boxing career. I wrote to him, explaining everything and he agreed to write the foreword on behalf of him and Ali. If you're going to dream, make it a big one.

Ultimately, if you are reading this book and have read up to this point, I want to offer you my sincerest thanks for being a part of my dream (and sparing Geraldine any more of those annoying holiday conversations). If you do follow the principles in it and it helps you achieve your dreams, please tell me about it. That will be an affirmation of my purpose. Which is where we started this book...

Thanks for reading. Now it's your turn

Damian.
Port Sunlight, October 2005.

Bibliography (in alphabetical order, according to author)

'Den of Lions', *Terry Anderson.*
Anderson was an American who was held hostage at the same time as Keenan and McCarthy. His story is equally compelling although he was a man who invested his faith in natural justice and believed that he would be freed as he had done nothing wrong. His dignity and faith are astounding. I once met Anderson. He maintains that we could all survive his ordeal as "we do not know just how capable we are until forced to prove it."

'It's not about the bike' and 'Every second counts', *Lance Armstrong.*
Two books that should be on every school curriculum. The first book details his upbringing and how this forged his love of cycling and competition and then covers his fight with cancer and how he beat this and then went on to win his first Tour de France. The second book is about his life after this and the longer term impact which cancer has had on his life and the lessons and changes it has had on him. Brilliant.

'Mourinho: Anatomy of a Winner', *Patrick Barclay.*
A fascinating profile of Jose Mourinho, looking at how he started out in coaching and refined his skills along with his mental approach to become one of the most successful modern-era coaches.

'The Butterfly and the Diving Bell', *Jean-Dominique Bauby.*
This is the story of man who suffered from a massive stroke and then came round to find himself suffering from a condition known as 'locked in syndrome'. The only method of communication was to move his left eyelid. This book is amazing on a few levels. Firstly, Bauby wrote it by spelling out every letter. Secondly, it's a book that describes in rich, evocative detail the simple things, which we take for granted. Beautiful.

'Don't Die with the Music in you', *Wayne Bennett.*
A short book written by the legendary Australian Rugby League coach, which touches on sport, life and his own values which have inspired him to success.

'The Gate', *Francois Bizot.*
Harrowing account of man who was captured by Khmer Rouge soldiers in Cambodia yet emerged to become a powerful intermediary in the civil war.

'The 90 minute manager', *David Bolchover and Chris Brady.*
A great book which contains a lot of research into how football can provide lots of lessons for the world of work.

'Losing my Virginity', *Sir Richard Branson.*
A good book describing how he built up his business empire along with great insights into the attitudes and beliefs that have made him so successful.

'The Disney Way', *Bill Capodagli and Lynn Jackson.*
A book which describes how the Disney empire was established and how it has adapted to still maintain its success today.

'The Disney Way Fieldbook', *Bill Capodagli and Lynn Jackson.*
A series of exercises which Disney use to train its staff.

'How to win friends and influence people', *Dale Carnegie.*
This is an old book but is regarded as a classic. It has lots of tips and advice about how to work effectively with others.

'The 13th Round', *Rubin Carter.*
'Hurricane' Carter was a potential world boxing champion until he was given life imprisonment for a murder he maintains he did not commit. This book tells, in graphic detail, of his brutal upbringing in young offenders prisons and his subsequent fight for justice and how he fought for his beliefs .

'Go!', *Barbara Cassani.*
A great book which covers the start up of the budget airline and how it involved and inspired its staff.

'The Boss', *Michael Crick.*
This is a great counter-balance into Ferguson's own account of his life and times. It presents others insights, both good and bad, into Ferguson and his qualities.

'Creativity flow and the psychology of discovery and invention', *Mihaly Csikszentmihalyi.*
A book detailing the science behind creativity.

'Winning', *Frank Dick.*
This is a short book written by one of the best sports coaches of the last 30 years. Frank Dick uses his experience of coaching the cream of British athletics to provide insights into how these lessons can be used in our own lives to succeed in what we want to achieve.

'I only talk winning', *Angelo Dundee.*
The book by Muhammad Ali and Sugar Ray Leonard's trainer offers some great insights into the mentality required to be a success in both the boxing ring and in life.

'A Strange Kind of Glory', *Eamon Dunphy.*
The best biography of Sir Matt Busby ever written. This book offers a great view into Busby's vision of a successful football club, which upheld his own values of honesty, ambition, excitement with the accent on developing young talent, along with his attempts to create it. Values which are still steeped into the core of the club today.

'Walt Disney: Hollywood's Dark Prince', *Marc Elliot.*
An alternative view of Disney, which has a lot of research on his upbringing which helped shape his character.

'The wicked wit of Winston Churchill', *Dominique Enright.*
A series of quotes from Churchill. Worth having to hand for if you ever find yourself short of something to say.

'They made America: from the steam to the search engine', *Sir Harold Evans.*
A book about America's pioneers.

'Man's search for meaning', *Victor Frankl.*
The book of learnings compiled by Frankl, who survived the Nazi concentration camps. This is a powerful and moving book and I'd advocate everyone to read it.

'They did; you can', *Michael Finnigan.*
A collection of fascinating interviews with everyday people who were inspired to achieve their own goals. If you have enjoyed my book, you will love this one.

'Managing my life', *Sir Alex Ferguson.*
Whatever you think of Ferguson, you can't deny his passion, ambition, drive and fierce will-to-win along with his values of loyalty and commitment. This book explains how these were formed to help him achieve unprecedented success.

'The Life and Times of Muhammad Ali', *Thomas Hauser.*
One of the best biographies of all-time. This book is the most comprehensive account of Ali you could find. Read about his rise to become world heavyweight champion, his refusal to go to Vietnam, his re-emergence as champ and his subsequent life after boxing. This book is brilliant.

'How to be brilliant!', *Michael Heppell.*
Does what it says on the cover! A book that offers advice on how to reach your goals.

'Success through a positive mental attitude', *Napolean Hill and W. Clement Stone.*
Stone built $100 into a multi-million dollar organisation and he describes the techniques he used to achieve this.

'Starmaker', *Brian Hughes MBE.*
The definitive book on Jimmy Murphy, Sir Matt Busby's assistant. Packed with anecdotes about how Murphy's revolutionary coaching and motivational techniques helped to nurture the finest collection of footballers ever, 'the Busby Babes'. This is a book written by my hero about one of my heroes.

'Who moved my cheese?', *Dr Spencer Johnson.*
An book which contains lots of home truths told within a story about two mice searching for cheese. Sounds unusual? It is, but worth a read.

'A flame of pure fire – Jack Dempsey and the roaring 20's', *Roger Khan*
An excellent book which looks at the social implications of early 20th century America and the Depression which was the emergence of Jack Dempsey, a lad that grew up homeless and without a base to become the world heavyweight champion.

'Churchill', *Roy Jenkins*.
Biography of Britain's great war time leader. It is a compelling book.

'An Evil Cradling', *Brian Keenan*.
This is one of my favourite books of all-time and Keenan is one of my ultimate heroes. He was taken as a hostage in Beirut in the mid-1980's and held for 5 years. In the book, he describes how, despite having his basic needs denied, he manages to retain his values of honour, respect and dignity. Keenan says about the book:

"I try to illustrate what happens to the mind...when a man seeks desperately to unite vision and will by whatever power is within him, how adversity is overcome. The process is long and awful."

Those are not two words which you could use to describe this classic.

'Bob Paisley – Manager of the Millennium', *John Keith*.
Similar to the Eamon Dunphy book on Busby, this is a comprehensive study of Liverpool's most successful manager and gives a great insight into his values and beliefs along with his determination to maintain the success he enjoyed.

'Sven', *Joe Lovejoy*.
A biography of the England manager, covering his early coaching career in Sweden and Portugal.

'Taking on the World', *Ellen MacArthur*.
The youngest and also the fastest woman to sail, single-handedly, round the world. She tells her story with real honesty, sharing her fears and doubts, which allows the reader to get a real understanding into the mind and motivation of someone who possess a certainty of what she wants and how she is going to get it.

'Long walk to freedom', *Nelson Mandela*.
Mandela's own autobiography. Fascinating insight into how he maintained his dignity and challenged his anger into finding a solution to apartheid.

'Some Other Rainbow', *John McCarthy and Jill Morrell*.
John McCarthy was held as a hostage with Keenan for 4 of the 5 years he was in captivity. His story is equally amazing, as he retains his own quiet dignity in the face of horrendous circumstances. His partner, Jill Morrell campaigned to get the British government to act for his release. This is a brilliant book to show just how powerful passion and belief is and how it can sustain you beyond what you believe are your own limits.

'How to be a complete and utter failure in life, work and everything', *Steve McDermott*.
A fantastic and compelling book, which is packed with facts, anecdotes and philosophies told in an easy-to-read and conversational style which, if you ignore and disregard, can help you succeed in failing!

'S.U.M.O (Shut Up and Move On)', *Paul McGee*.
A fun and illuminating book which provides a no-nonsense set of tips.

'Jock Stein', *Archie McPherson*.
Alex Ferguson's hero. This book is a brilliant biography of Scotland's greatest manager. Imagine a team winning the European Cup with 11 local lads. This book explains how Stein made this happen.

'The Iceman', *John Monie*
A fascinating book about the life and coaching expertise of the legendary Rugby League coach, John Monie.

'Just say a few words', *Bob Monkhouse*.
A brilliant book by the late comedian, which contains loads of tips about public speaking, including an excellent chapter of how to handle your own doubts and 'self-talk' before standing up at an important event. Plus, it's got loads of funny stories, anecdotes and one-liners.

'One Step Beyond', *Chris Moon*.
This is the inspiring story of a man who believed he could make a difference. After leaving the military, he went to Cambodia to help clear landmines and was captured by Khmer Rouge rebels. He later went to Mozambique and was blown up by a mine, losing his leg and arm. Within a year of this, he ran the London Marathon and within 3 years, he had run across the Sahara Desert. An amazing testimony to the power of the mind to overcome the steepest odds.

'Linus Pauling; Advancing Science, Advocating Peace',
Naomi Pasachoff.
A biography of the two-time Nobel prize winner, Pauling was an activits against atomic weapons and was subsequently accused of being a communist and suffered persecution, yet maintained his beliefs in spite of huge pressure.

'The power of positive thinking',
Norman Vincent Peale.
More practical tips which provide you with the tools to carry out your ambitions and hopes.

'A lifetime in a race',
Sir Matthew Pinsent.
A revealing sporting autobiography that offers insights into the mind of the athletes. Pinsent talks candidly about his own doubts and fears and how he dealt with them to win 4 Olympic gold medals.

'Still Me', *Christopher Reeve.*
This book, by the former 'Superman' actor recounts his tragic horse-riding accident and tells his life and career story up until then in a series of flashback sequences. There are some heart-breaking descriptions of how he came to terms with suffering from complete paralysis and being unable to breathe without support. His determination to defy doctors and learn to walk again, in order to be able to play with his young son is an amazing testimony to the power of belief. Although he didn't walk before his death, he did successfully gain funding into research and pioneered many techniques which will, one day, enable others to walk again. It is inspiring and very motivating.

'Mandela', *Anthony Sampson.*
The definite biography of Mandela. Offers comprehensive views of him from others' perspectives.

'Touching the void', *Joe Simpson.*
An awesome story of survival in the mountains. This book has become regarded as a climbers' classic.

'The legacy of Alfred Nobel',
Ragnar Sohlman.
The story of how the inventor of dynamite chose to leave a legacy that was intended to celebrate and help secure peace.

'After the Ball', *Nobby Stiles*
This is an excellent book by Stiles, a World and European Cup winner. He describes how he battled against huge odds to become a footballing legend, whilst still maintaining the values he grew up with. Inspiring and illuminating.

'Khrushchev', *William Taubman.*
Biography of Russian leader.

'Jack', *Jack Welch*
The autobiography of the head of GE. An excellent book written in a down-to-earth manner, which makes it really accessible to all.

'Feel', *Robbie Williams.*
Autobiography of the pop singer, charting his life and career.

'The Luck Factor',
Richard Wiseman.
Explanations of the science behind what can sometimes appear to be random or lucky events with lots of tips about how you can also become 'lucky'.

'Winning!', *Sir Clive Woodward.*
This book really appealed to me as it combined the worlds of sport with lessons which can be adapted and applied to the workplace. Don't let his subsequent failure with the British Lions and his transfer to football put you off. There is lots in this book which anyone can learn from.

'Raising kids in a negative world',
Zig Ziglar.
A must for all parents. Packed with lots of tips, help and advice about raising kids and about seeing the very best in them.

'The Mind Gym'.
This book captures a lot of the information found at the website of the same name. It is best read in sections and is packed with lots of easy to understand scientific data which explains our behaviours and attitudes and has loads of tips about how we can improve.

Testimonies

Nobby Stiles is one of only two Englishmen to have won the World Cup and the European Cup. The other is Sir Bobby Charlton.

I am honoured to be asked to contribute to this book and I hope that it provides you with some insights and inspiration which will let you go on and achieve your dreams and ambitions, just as I achieved mine by playing for Manchester United, winning the European Cup in 1968 and winning the World Cup with England in 1966.

I grew up in the back streets of Collyhurst, Manchester and my poor eyesight, lack of height and slight frame made me possibly the least likeliest contender to ever achieve footballing fame. I did it, however, through a combination of knowing what my dream was and never losing sight of it, no matter how tough times got, and by having a fierce determination to succeed. Without these attributes, all of the skill in the world wouldn't have helped me and it is for this reason that I'd encourage you to read this book and have a go at the exercises that are at the end of each chapter.

I would have loved the chance to read a book that could have helped me take a step closer towards my ambitions when I was younger and you should also make the most of the chances which are offered to you in this book.

On that famous day in June 1966, just before extra-time in the World Cup Final, Sir Alf Ramsey told us that we had the chance to step forward and achieve our ambitions over the next 30 minutes. We met the challenge that day and this book presents you with the same opportunity to understand and achieve your own ambitions. Make sure you take it.

Nobby Stiles MBE

Chris Moon MBE was captured in Cambodia by the Khmer Rouge and is one of the few westerners to survive. He was then blown up by a land mine and lost an arm and a leg. Less than a year after leaving hospital, he ran the London Marathon. He has since ran 250 kms across the Sahara, 5 back-to-back marathons across Death Valley (twice!) and climbed Mount Kilimanjaro.

Why Bother?...It's always easier to do nothing

I can't be bothered, I can't be arsed, it's too much effort, I don't read, I'm just biding my time, so why should I read this book?

This is a great book and the reason this book should be read is because it's an injection of positive energy- pure, prime nutrition for the brain. It'll be good for you... You can do more than you think... Broaden your horizons.

I've had the good fortune to visit some unusual places, such as countries emerging from civil war and I was working to clear the debris of war- landmines and unexploded ordnance in Mozambique East Africa when I was blown up losing two limbs. I mention this because it has taught me a great deal.

Firstly, I believe we have so much we take for granted. You shouldn't have to lose something to appreciate its value. Things are changing fast in the modern world. We need to cope with change and recognize we may not be able to stay in the same place if the world is moving on around us. So I had to learn to manage the change and I did this by being open-minded and being prepared to see things from a different perspective.

That's why I believe this book is important. It's all about doing and living life, rather than sitting there and letting life do it to you. In the modern corporate world I find it refreshing that Damian Hughes has written this book which is a bit like a road atlas for life, so well done for reading it and remember you can do more than you think... Everyone can go one step beyond their limits.

Chris Moon MBE

Sir John Jones KBE has been a Head teacher of three secondary schools over a period of 17 years, including the worst performing school in the UK. He was successful in turning around the performance and was awarded a knighthood for his services to education in 2003.

The world is full of heroes and our lives are enriched with stories of heroism and heroic deeds.

We all need our legends. However, true heroism is not confined to such places as battlefields or sports arenas. It is found mostly in the day to day deeds of ordinary people performing them extraordinarily well. This book gives tribute to such people.

Look around you at home, in the community, on the shop floor, in the workshop and in the office - they are there, showing courage, passion, resilience and the will never to give up, whatever the challenge.

This book will probably surprise you, definitely move you, but mostly inspire you. Perhaps in reading it you will find the courage to be heroic in your own life.

Read it, enjoy it and be inspired!

Sir John Jones

Wayne Bennett was an international rugby league footballer in the 1970's and has been the coach of the Brisbane Broncos since 1988. Before that, he was co-coach of the Canberra Raiders. He has won 5 Premiership titles and had outstanding success at State of Origin level, leading Queensland to victory on four occasions. He is also the national team coach. He is the author of the best selling book, 'Don't die with the music in you'. Wayne Bennett is an Australian sporting legend.

There are two quotes which I use a lot and think they neatly summarise the content of this book.

"If it's to be, it's up to me"

and

"People don't fail in life, they just give up trying".

Use this book to teach yourself never to accept your second best.

Wayne Bennett

Daley Thompson claims more decathlon honours than anyone before or after him. He is the first person to hold World, Olympic, Commonwealth and European Championships titles in the same year as well as a world record. Daley was unbeaten in nine years and was the Olympic Champion in 1980 and 1984, World Champion in 1983, European Champion in 1982 and 1986, and the Commonwealth Champion in 1978, 1982 and 1986. He held four world records in his career. Daley was awarded a CBE in 2000 and was voted BBC sports personality of the year in 1982.

As a double Olympic decathlon Champion, I am fully aware of the demands that are required to be the best and achieve your dreams. I am very familiar with the tips, skills and techniques demonstrated and I recommend that you take some time and sit and read this book. The skills taught can be invaluable and if applied could change your life!

Daly Thompson.

Jonny Wilkinson, a fly-half for England Rugby Union and one of the most famous players in international professional rugby, was catapulted to stardom when his drop goal during extra time won England the World Cup in 2003. Wilkinson made his debut in 1998, joining the Newcastle Falcons (his local club) and England Rugby Union. On the field he has a reputation for accurate kicking and fierce tackling; off the field he has a reputation for practising incessantly and avoiding publicity. After his dramatic role in the 2003 World Cup victory, Wilkinson became a national hero in England, was named the BBC Sports Personality of the Year and awarded the Order of the British Empire and was named captain of England's team.

Setting yourself challenges and goals in life, particularly when life is not treating you well, is a positive reaction to what are more often than not, very negative circumstances.

I am lucky enough to lead a very happy and privileged life through the love and support of my friends and family. However, in the world of life and rugby I have some very clear and definite principles. I firmly believe that you only get out of life what you put into it and striving to improve your circumstances and achieve your goals gives so much more satisfaction than sitting back and letting life pass you by. One day you may live to regret it.

I have some sayings which I look to when things do not seem to be going so well either on the rugby pitch or off it and which Damian has captured the essence of in this excellent book. Some of these are:

'Destiny is no matter of chance. It is a matter of choice.' (*William Jennings Byran*)

'A person who aims at nothing is sure to hit it.' (*Anon*)

'I play the odds – the harder I work, the more likely I am to succeed.'

'Challenges are what make life interesting; overcoming them is what makes life meaningful.' (*Joshua J Marine*)

'I can't always succeed but I can always deserve to.'

Clearly you are lucky enough to have some very kind, caring and hard working people around you and I wish them, and especially you readers, the very best of luck in the future.

Jonny Wilkinson

Acknowledgements

This book wouldn't have been possible without the help of so many people. I'd like to offer my sincerest thanks to each of them and my apologies to anyone who I have inadvertently missed.

Geraldine, this book only exists because of your help, patience, advice, support and feedback. You don't know just how much you mean to me. Thanks for inspiring me.

Mum and Dad. Thanks for the encouragement, advice and constant inspiration. My heroes.

Chris, the best mate I could have.

Anthony and Rachael, thanks for the encouragement and web surfing.

Mari and Gerry, your attention to detail was phenomenal and your support vital. Thanks.

Chris Mallaband, the inventor of Liquid Thinking. Thanks mate.

Phil Ince, the embodiment of Liquid Thinking. Thanks for being pernickety!

Iain and Andrea Allen, thanks for taking the time out from your own masterpiece to help.

Tracy Pettitt, thanks for the encouragement. Sorry for disturbing your train journeys!

John E Roberts. You're going to be in the next one.

Kim and Pete Lewis. Thanks for backing the initial idea, even though you thought I'd lost it.

Emma Finlay. The advice and unfailing support was amazing and invaluable. Remember me when you're running the place!

Dave and Vicky Morgan. Your guidance and advice kept this book on course when it looked like getting lost. Vicky, apologies for keeping him working late to read the many drafts.

Lucia McCann, for supporting this concept.

Ben Jemison from www.leafinteractive.co.uk for helping set up www.liquidthinker.com

Nicky Wooton and Andrew Park from CognitiveMedia. Thanks for humouring me at Fouracres and backing the idea with your amazing support. Much appreciated.

Nobby Stiles MBE, Sir Richard Branson, Angelo Dundee, Sir John Jones, Chris Moon, Daley Thompson, Jonny Wilkinson and Wayne Bennett for offering your backing, support and encouragement.

Martin Perry for your great insights and challenges.

Mike Finnigan and 'Advance'.

Sue Schoormans for your support.

Sue and Georgia Roberts. Thanks for your encouragement and feedback.

Chris Lunt. Thanks for your advice and guidance.

Dr. Michael Cross. Thanks for listening and your advice.

Brian and Christine Higginson. Inspirational.

Paul Lee. Respect.

Mark Holden. Good luck with wedding.

Steve Byrne. What's next?

Gerry Fannon. Hope you and the boat make it to Ireland one day.

Andy Hardcastle. Please now say something nice about Human Racehorses.

Forza Malaka!

All Liquid Thinkers. Thanks for the inspiration.

About the author

Damian Hughes was born and raised in Manchester. He played football as a schoolboy for Nottingham Forest and England before studying Classics at Leeds University. He began working as a football coach for Bobby Charlton Soccer Schools and Manchester United. He later joined Unilever, in 2000, as a Human Resource Manager and has worked in Port Sunlight since 2004. He also works as a coach and volunteer at the Collyhurst and Moston Boxing Club in Manchester.